John Thomas Porter

# A System of Shorthand in Which the Vowels Are Expressed in the Consonant Stems by Making the Latter of Different Lengths

John Thomas Porter

**A System of Shorthand in Which the Vowels Are Expressed in the Consonant Stems by Making the Latter of Different Lengths**

ISBN/EAN: 9783337811877

Printed in Europe, USA, Canada, Australia, Japan

Cover: Foto ©Thomas Meinert / pixelio.de

More available books at **www.hansebooks.com**

# A

# SYSTEM OF SHORTHAND

## IN WHICH

## THE VOWELS ARE EXPRESSED IN THE

## CONSONANT STEMS

## BY MAKING THE LATTER OF DIFFERENT LENGTHS.

BY

JOHN T. PORTER, PITTSBURG, PA.

# STEM-VOWEL SHORTHAND.

Stem-Vowel Shorthand is a simple, scientific system without word-signs, in which the exact sound of every syllable is expressed with absolute accuracy by making the consonant stems of different lengths, and is the only method by which one person can read another's notes.

It has the unqualified approval of every stenographer who has ever EXAMINED it, and they all unanimously recommend it as the system for beginners.

The only opposition it is meeting with is from Principals of business colleges and their teachers of shorthand, whose business it is injuring.

Owing to the wonderful inventions of late years, however. both business and social life is undergoing a transformation, old methods are giving place to new, and those sticklers for ancient methods must either conform to the new order of things or find themselves brushed aside, and entirely out of the race in the great march of improvement.

The inventor of Stem-Vowel Shorthand, having been for many years a Graham writer, and an official reporter in the Courts of Pennsylvania, makes the following propositions :

First  That Stem-Vowel Shorthand HAS TEN PER CENT. FEWER MOVEMENTS OF THE PEN than any other system in the world.

Second. That it is 100 PER CENT. MORE EASILY LEARNED to the same degree of proficiency.

Third.  That it is 500 PER CENT. MORE LEGIBLE.

To give force and effect to these propositions. the inventor of Stem-Vowel Shorthand will give $1,000 to any one who will show them to be untrue.

Mr. Porter is a substantial real estate owner of Pittsburg and can be held legally responsible for his assertions, if they are not true.

. The average time required to attain a speed of 100 words per minute is five months.  During the past year a number of pupils reached that state of efficiency in three and four months—notably, Mrs. Alice Davis. who learned in three months. and took a position with Jos  Horne & Co , a firm employing none but the most skilled employes ; Miss Nora Kohn. who learned in four months, and took a position with the law firm of Marshall & Sproul. and Miss Anna Nolan, who learned in four months, and took a position with the Commission House of Poth & Haberman.

Mr. Webster, one of the most efficient reporters in the Courts of Pittsburg, reached a speed of 200 words per minute in nine months from the time he commenced taking lessons.

# PORTER'S SCHOOL OF STEM-VOWEL SHORTHAND.

TERMS.

The terms are eight dollars per month, in advance, for day sessions, commencing at 9 A. M. and ending at 3 P. M.

Evening sessions five dollars per month, from 6 to 9:30 P. M.

Scholarships, $40.

As the instruction to beginners is strictly personal, pupils may enter at any time, their month being computed from the date of enrollment.

As many persons are not adapted to the study or practice of shorthand, it would be as foolish for them to undertake to learn it, as it would be for a lady without an ear for music to undertake to make a music teacher of herself.

In order to insure success, pupils will be taken on trial for a month without charge. If they develop a taste for the study, and are adapted to it in other ways, they will be finally enrolled as pupils.

If, at the end of the month, pupils are not pleased, or the teacher gives an unfavorable decision as to their fitness, they drop the study, without any expense except the cost of writing material, and the loss of time

Books are furnished without charge, and writing material will cost the pupil from ten to fifteen cents per week.

Porter's Stem-Vowel Shorthand, Part First, containing the system complete, FOR SELF INSTRUCTION, price $1.00.

NOTE.—The publication of Porter's Stem-Vowel Shorthand represents a new departure in book-making.

Every page of the book, except the shorthand, was printed on the typewriter by a pupil in the school. A photo-engraved plate, reduced one-third in size, was then made of each page and the book was printed from those plates.

# PREFACE.

The wheels of progress are rolling onward. The age of steam is passing away, and the era of electricity is dawning. The wonderful inventions of past decades are being supplanted by the still more wonderful inventions of the present. Old methods must give place to new, in spite of the prejudice and bigotry that would prevent progress.

The old methods of shorthand that answered the purpose of parliamentary and congressional reporting a quarter of a century ago do not meet the demands of the commercial world of the present, which requires a system easily learned, easily read and brief enough to record the most rapid utterance. The profession is crowded at the bottom with so-called stenographers who will always stay at the bottom, from their inability, with the means at their command, to rise above it; while the favored few, who, by dint of long years of patient toil, have reached the higher walks of the profession, are reaping rich rewards from their skill.

In presenting this book to the public, I may say at the outset that the system of shorthand embodied in it is not a mere rehash or improvement, as is the case with nearly all others, of the old Pitman system, but that it is founded upon an entirely different theory; that it contains no word-signs, or arbitrary characters; that it is fully vocalized, rendering it as easily read as the common long-hand script; and that, from the simplicity of its construction, it is as easily learned as the common long-hand writing.

In regard to speed, it has been already demonstrated beyond peradventure that it excels the most rapid of the old methods. In writing testimony, one hundred and fifty movements of the pen make one hundred words, and this fact, in connection with the very limited amount of shading, or heavy strokes, make it capable of meeting the highest requirements of speed.

Having used the Pitman-Graham methods of shorthand for many years as official reporter in the courts of Pennsylvania, I may be permitted to claim a thorough knowledge of the subject. If the interested student will give this book a careful examination, he will find in it a system of shorthand scientific from the first principle to the last, easily learned, easily read, and entirely free from the word-signs and arbitrary characters which burden the older systems.

The system is complete in this one volume, the subject-matter and its arrangements being the result of long experience in teaching shorthand. The lessons are arranged in progressive order, leading the student by easy steps through the principles, into commercial letter-writing, deeds, mortgages, specifications, testimony, etc., so that, having made himself master of the subject-matter of the book, he is thoroughly prepared to perform any branch of the stenographic work.

A word in regard to the time required to master the contents of the book. I am warranted, by an experience of three years in teaching Stem-Vowel Shorthand, in saying, that a pupil of ordinary ability can easily reach a speed of one hundred words per minute in a very few months of earnest, decided attention and practice. Of course, a higher rate of speed will require the same diligence for a longer period.

The system suggests its own name, Stem-Vowel Shorthand, from the fact that the vowels are expressed by different lengths of the consonant stems, instead of by extra marks as in the older systems.

In conclusion, I may add that the high state of proficiency reached by the army of stenographers in this city and through the United States, who use the Stem-Vowel Shorthand, the responsible positions filled by them, and their high encomiums of the system, are extremely gratifying to me, and give abundant assurance that my labors in this field have opened the way to a state of proficiency in the art, scarcely attainable through the devious windings of the old method.

JOHN T. PORTER.

## PREFACE TO SECOND EDITION.

The second edition of Stem-Vowel Shorthand contains some radical improvements over the system as set forth in the first edition. The placing of the hooks and circles on the right of stems to indicate the first group of vowels, and on the left to indicate the second group, is attended with surprising results in regard to legibility and ease of learning.

The improvements have all been made in the direction of simplicity, and have resulted in reducing the number of lessons by about one-third.

Bountiful Nature has been very prodigal of her wonderful secrets of late years, and the transition from the era of steam to the era of electricity requires old methods to conform to the new order of things, or else stand aside and let modern methods take their places.

The author believes that Stem-Vowel Shorthand will meet the requirements of the times in regard to speed, ease of learning and legibility, and will go hand in hand with sister sciences as vehicles for the rapid transaction of business.

THE AUTHOR.

July 1st, 1896.

# PART FIRST.

## CHAPTER I.

## PRELIMINARY.

Stem-vowel Shorthand,or Phonography,is both a science and an art.

Considered by itself,wholly separate and apart from the purposes to which it is adapted,it is a science,being a body of principles arranged in systematic order.

When practical skill is accquired to apply these principles to the purpose for which the system is designed,Stem-Vowel Shorthand becomes an art.

The system is purely phonetic in its character,being founded upon the elementary sounds of the human voice,which are retained without modification when the system is applied to the art of writing.

The elementary sounds of the human voice are of three kinds,distinguished as vowels,consonants,and diphthongs.

The vowels are twelve in number.-- six long,and six short, and three diphthongs.

## LONG VOWELS.

| FIRST GROUP. | SECOND GROUP. |
|---|---|
| Ē,as in ear. | AW,as in law. |
| Ā," " air. | Ō," " lo,or go. |
| Ă," " are. | OŌ," " loot or boot. |

THIRD GROUP.
Diphthongs.
Ī,as in ire.
OI," " oil.
OW," " how.

The pupil should drill himself thoroughly on the three groups until he has mastered them.

Perfect familiarity with all the vowel sounds in their order will make phonetic spelling a pleasure rather than a task.

# CONSONANTS.

T D, P B, K Gay, F V, Ch, J, S Z, W, M N, TH.

/ ⟋ ⏌ ⟍ ⟍ ⟋ ⏋ ⏌ ⟋

## THE CONSONANT T.

| FIRST GROUP. | SECOND GROUP. | THIRD GROUP. |
|---|---|---|
| Ē, Ā, Ä. | AW, Ō, OO. | Ī, OI, OW. |
| tē, tā, tah. | taw, toe, too. | tie, toi, tou. |

In the line above, the consonant stem T is divided into three different lengths, to correspond to the three different vowels in each group.

Give to each length of the consonant stem in the first group the sound indicated by the vowel above it, -- the shortest length Ē, the middle length Ā, the longest Ä.

The second group stems are distinguished from the first and the third group by having the heavy dot on the left of the stems.

The diphthongs are shaded lightly.

Write the T stems in each group a great many times, pronouncing each stem as you write it.

## THE S CIRCLE.

The initial and final consonant S is represented by a small circle, beginning or ending the stem on the right-hand side in the first and the third group, and on the left side of the stems in the second group.

tēse, tāse, tās.   taws, tose, toos.   tise, tois, tous.

stē, stā, stah.   staw, stow, stoo.   stie, stoi, stou.

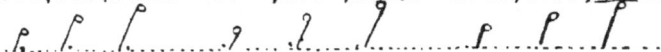

stēse, stāse, stas.   staws, stose, stoos.   sties, stois, stous

The final syllable SES is indicated by extending the S circle through the stem and forming an additional S on the opposite side.

teases,taises,tosses.    tosses,toases,tooses.

*[shorthand symbols]*

## THE L AND THE R HOOK.

The consonant L, as an initial and final, is represented by
a small hook joined to the right side of the stems in the
first and the third group, and to the left of the stems in the
second group.

tēle,tãle,täl.    tawl,tole,tool.    tile,toil,toul.

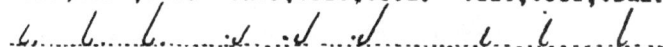

*[shorthand symbols]*

stele,stale,stal,    stawl,stole,stool.    stile,stoil,stoul.

*[shorthand symbols]*

The consonant R is represented by a hook twice as large
as the L hook.

tere,tare,tar.    tawr,tore,toor.    tire,toir,tour.

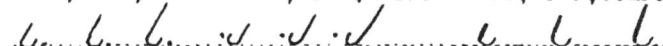

*[shorthand symbols]*

stere,stare,star.    stawr,store,stoor.    stire,stoir,stour.

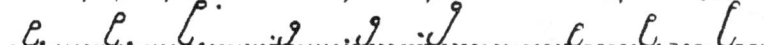

*[shorthand symbols]*

The final circles are made inside the hooks.

tears,tairs,tars.    tawrs,toars,toors.    tires,toirs,tours.

*[shorthand symbols]*

teals,tails,tals.    tawls,toals,tools.    tiles,toils,touls

*[shorthand symbols]*

## READING AND WRITING EXERCISE.

Analyze each word in the following exercise, and then
write the whole exercise a number of times, pronouncing each
word as you write it; thus:
Tea, a word of the first group, first length, dot on right
of stem.
Tow, a word of the second group, second length, dot on left
of stem.

Too, a word of the second group, third length, dot on left of stem.

Tie, a word of the third group, first length dot on right of stem.

Tease, a word of the first group, first length, S circle on right of stem.

Taws, a word of the second group, first length, S circle on left of stem.

Remember that the shorthand character represents the sound of a word, and not its English spelling.

Tea, tease, stay, teases, teal, tale, steal, stale, tear, tare, tar, stear, stare, star, teals, tales, tears, tares, stairs, stars, tow, too, taws, toes, stow, stew, tosses, tall, stews, stole, stool, stall, tore, tour, store, tools, stools, stalls, tie, toy, ties, toys, sties, tile, toil, towel, style, tire, tower, tiles towels, styles, A.

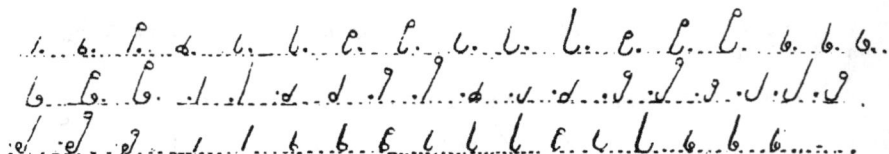

Go through the exercise again, analyzing each shorthand character, and writing it in long-hand. Do the same with all the following lessons in the principles.

### SENTENCES.

A tall stool. A steel tool. A tall toy. A tall tower. A tile tore a towel. A steel tower. A stale store. A tall tar stole a store. Toss a toy to a tower. 'Tow a star to a tower.

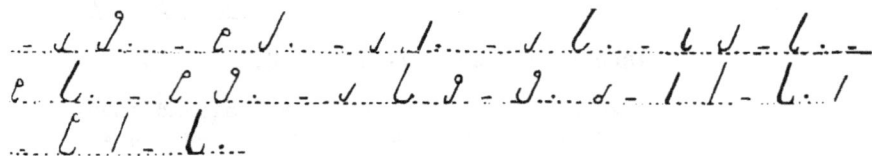

## CHAPTER II.

### SHORT VOWELS.

| FIRST GROUP. | SECOND GROUP. |
|---|---|
| ĭ,as in ik,or lick. | ŏ,as in ok,or lock. |
| ĕ,'"  " ek,or leck. | ŭ, "  " uk,or luck. |
| ă, "  " ak,or lack. | ŏŏ, "  " ook,or look. |

As will be seen above,each group of long vowels has a
corresponding group of short vowels.

The stems having the short sounds are distinguished from
those having the long sounds by a very light dot at the side
of the stem.

Rapid progress will be impossible without a thorough
knowledge of the long and the short vowel sounds. Write each
group at least ten times,pronouncing the word represented by
the stem as you write it.

FIRST GROUP.
tĭs,tĕs,tăs.

SECOND GROUP.
tŏs,tŭs,tŏŏs.

stĭs,stĕs,stăs.

stŏs,stŭs,stŏŏs.

tĭl,tĕl,tăl.

tŏl,tŭl,tŏŏl.

stĭl,stĕl,stăl.

stŏl,stŭl,stŏŏl.

Observe that the first long and the first short vowel of
the second group are alike in many words.

The initial and final consonant N is represented by a small circle twice as large as the S circle.

tēne,tāne,tan.    tawn,tone,tōon.    tine,toin,toun,

tĭn,tĕn,tăn.    tŏn,tŭn,tōon.

stēne,stāne,stan.    stawn,stone,stōon.    stine,stoin,stoun.

stĭn,stĕn,stăn.    stŏn,stŭn,stōon.

The initial and final M is represented by a circle twice as large as the N circle.

tēme,tāme,tăm.    tawm,tome,tōom.    time,toim,toum.

tĭm,tĕm,tăm.    tŏm,tŭm,tōom.

steme,stame,stăm.    stom,stome,stōom.    stime,stoim,stoum.

The final N and the final M circle take the S circle on the opposite side of the stem.

teens,tains,tĕns.    tawns,tones,tōons.    tines,toins,touns.

Final F or V is represented by a small curve at the end of the stem.

tĭf,tĕf,tăf.    tŏf,tŭf,tōof.

The nasal sound ING or INK is represented by a small curve on the end of a hook or stem;thus;

tilling,telling,talling.    tolling,tulling,tooling.

ting,teng,tang.    tong,tung,toong.

teasing,taising,tassing.    tossing,toasing,toosing,etc.

The final syllables RY and LY are represented by a small vertical or horizontal tick on the end of the R and the L hook, thus:

tilly,telly,tally.    tolly,tully,tooly.

teary,tairy,tarry.    tawry,tory,toory.

Practice analyzing and writing the following exercises until they can be written easily and readily from dictation. Write slowly and carefully,using the utmost care to make your writing accurate.

In writing the sentences,omit the dots entirely,as their only use is to aid the pupil in acquiring the ability to spell phonetically.

In words like tall,stall,toss,taws,etc.,either the long or the short sound may be used.

## READING AND WRITING EXERCISE

Tis,toss,till,tell,still,tan,tin,tone,tune,stone,stain, steam,team,tame,tomb,times,steams,stem,teams,stills,tans,tons, tough,tiff,stuff,staff,stiff,turf,tong,tongue,sting,tank,tally tilly,tarry,tory,story,starry,tilling,telling,tolling,tiling, toiling,toweling,tearing,storing,staring,stearing,teasing, tossing.

For the purpose of facilitating sentence-writing the following words selected from advanced lessons should be learned.

The, not, are, in, of, was, a or an, and, is, for.

*[shorthand notation]*

Stay in the store. 'Tis not the **time** for the star. Tell not tales to the stars. The tiles tore the towels. Time tells tales. Tools are in the store in town. Steam stains the tin in the tower. A towel and a stool, not a stone and a star. The team was not in time. Tell the tale in time. The style was not in time. The stuff was still tough. The teams are not in town. The staff is in the tower. The steam stains a ton of the stuff. The tongue is still. The stem was still stiff and tough. The stars tell a tale of time. Stow the stale stuff in the store. The tar was telling the story to the tory. For a time the stool was turning. The tiling was for the tall tower.

*[shorthand notation]*

# CHAPTER III

## TRANSPOSITION OF THE VOWEL.

When the stem is written across the line,the vowel expressed by the length of the stem precedes the consonant instead of following it,as in the preceding lessons.

ēte,āte,at.　awt,ote,ŏot.　ite,oit,out.

Observe that the dots,used to indicate the difference between the long and the short sounds,are placed at the beginning of the stems to show that the vowels come first.

īt,ĕt,àt.　　ŏt,ŭt,ŏŏt.

īts,ĕts,āts.　ŏts,ŭts,ŏŏts.

If the S circle begins the stems ēte,ate,at,etc.they become sete,sate,sat,etc.

sēte,sāte,sat.　sawt,sŏte,sŏot.　site,soit,sout.

Re-write giving the short sounds to the stems above.

sētes,sāits,sāts.　sawts,sŏats,sŏots.　sites,soits,souts.

sēten,sāten,sätten.　sŏtten,sŏten,sŏŏten.　siten,soiten,e

lēte,lāte,lät.　lŏt,lŏte,lŏot.　lite,loit,lout.

līt,lĕt,lăt.   lŏt,lŭt,lōͻt.

rete.rate,rát.   rot,rote,rōͻt.   rite,roit,rout.

rĭt,rĕt,răt.   rŏt,rŭt,rōͻt.

note,nate,nät.   not,note,nōͻt.   nite,noit,nout.

mete,mate,mät.   mot,mote,mōͻt.   mite,moit,mout.

meatle,maitle,mättle.   mottle,moetle,mōͻtle.   etc.

meter,maiter,mätter.   motter,moter,mōͻter.   etc.

leater,leiter,lätter.   lotter,loater,lōͻter.   etc.

Re-write the last five lines above,giving the short
sounds.

sĭttel,sĕttel,săttel.   sŏttel,sŭttel,sōͻtel.

netel,natel,nättel.   nottel,notel,nōͻotel.   nitel,noitel

nĭttel,nĕttel,năttel.   nŏttel,nŭttel,nōͻtel.

Begin the S circle with the L hook on the opposite side
for the double consonant SL.

slete.slate,slĕt.   slot .slote.slōͻt.   slite.sloit.etc.

# READING AND WRITING EXERCISE.

CAUTION.-- Write the following exercises of words and
sentences through four or five times. The more thoroughly
one lesson is learned, the easier the next lesson becomes.
Avoid efforts for speed. Write slowly and carefully.

Eat, ate, out, it, ought, eats, its, outs, seats, sat, set, loot, let
light, rate, rat, rot, rut, rout, meat, mot, suit, soot, sight, sit,
right, writ, wrought, sots, suits, sitter, setter, late, lot, lit, mote
mottle, nut, night, neat, mate, moot, might, mit, metel, meter, metter,
mutter, matters, meters, letters, little, mitten, satin, matin, rot-
ten, lighten, later, lighter, eating, meeting, sitting, items, out-
ing, matting, sleet, slate, slat, slot, slut, slit, slight.

The lights at night lighten toil. A rat ate the nuts in
the store. Stains of tears are in the letter. Stores ought
to meet the styles of the times. The light route was the
lighter at night. Settle the matter in time. Stay in town at
night. Set the matter right. Are the nights light? The
sight suits the time. The meat was not eaten. The tough sitter stays later. The stuff was stale. A light stain was in
the stuff. Store the stuff in the tower at night. Let the
tall sot settle the matter. The little letter was light. The
meeting was late at night. The little tools are neat. The
light metal was at the right rate.

# CHAPTER IV.

## THE CONSONANT D STEM.

The consonant D is distinguished from the T by a greater slant to the left. It takes the same initial and final consonants as the T stem.

dĕ,dă,däh.  daw,dŏe,dōo.  die,doi,dou.

dĕse,dāis,dës.  daws,dōes,dŏos.  dies,dois,dous.

dĭs,dĕs,dăs.  dŏs,dŭs,dōos.

dēle,dāle,däl.  dol,dōle,dool.  dile,doil,doul.

dĭl,dĕl,dăl.  dŏl.dŭl,dōol.

dĕre,dāre,där.  dor,dōre,door.  dire,doir,dour.

dĕne,dāne,dän.  don,dōne,dōon.  dine,doin,doun.

dĭn,dĕn,dăn.  dŏn,dŭn.dōon.

dĕme,dăme,däm.  dŏm,dōme,dōom.  dime,doim,doum.

dĭm,dĕm,dăm.  dŏm,dŭm.dōom.

ede,aid,ad.  od,ode,ood.  ide,oid,oud.

id,ed,ad.  od,ud,ood.

eder,ader,adder.  odder,oder,ooder.  ider,oider,ouder.

edel,aidel,addel.  oddel,odel,oodel.  idel,oidel,oudel.

seder,sader,sadder.  sodder,soder,sooder.  sider,soider,

Re-write the last three lines,giving the short sounds.

edem,aidem,addem.  oddem,oadem,oodem.  idem,oidem,oudem.

dinning,denning,danning.  donning,dunning,dooning.

ledel,laidel,laddel,  loddel,loadel,loodel.  lidel,etc.

leader,laider,ladder.  lodder,loader,looder.  lider,etc.

reader,raider,radder.  rodder,roader,rooder.  rider,etc.

nedel,naidel,naddel.  noddel,nodel,noodel.  nidel,etc.

middel,meddel,maddel.  moddel,muddel,noodel.

slid.sled,slod.  slod.slud,slood.

Re-write, giving the short sounds wherever necessary.

## READING AND WRITING EXERCISE.

Write all the words in the following exercise several
times from your knowledge of the principles, without referring
to the key below. Reverse the process, translate each shorthand character, and write it in long-hand.

Day, dough, do, die, days, doze, dunce, dice, deal, dole, dear, dare
door, dire, dower, dean, Dane, dan, din, den, done, dine, down, doom, dim,
dime, dumb, aid, add, odd, odder, oder, oders, adders, addle, seeds, sad,
sadder, sudden, lead, laid, load, lewd, lied, loud, leaders, leaden,
laden, louder, reads, reader, raid, raider, red, redden, rid, riddle,
saddle, sidle, led, saddles, dose, ding, raiding, leading, loading, dy-
ing, dining, dank, slid, sled, slide.

*[shorthand characters]*

A sudden light dims sight, dear reader. The leaders wrote
letters. A little lead settles at night. A dose of lead
might riddle the saddle of the rider. Dimes are not made of
tin. The leader was dumb. The dame was sad. The satin was
dear. The writer was not to tell the tale! The reader was
not to read the riddle. The load was laid in the road. The
right road to town was light. The load of turf is in the middle of the road. In the road was a load of lead. The metal
tank is down in the road.

*[shorthand characters]*

# CHAPTER V.

## THE DOUBLE CONSONANT ST.

To represent the double consonant ST.extend the S circle into a short,straight tick in the direction of the T stem.

teast,taist,tast.    tawst.toast.toost.    tiest,toist,etc.

Slanting the tick in the direction of the D stem changes the ST to SD.

teazd,taizd,tazd.    tawzd,toazd,toozd.    tiezd,toizd,touzd.

## THE TRIPLE CONSONANT STR.

The triple consonant STR is represented by adding the R hook to the tick.

teaster,taister,taster.    tawster.toaster,toaster.etc.

The short sounds of the lines above are,of course, indicated by making the dot very light.

## THE FINAL CONSONANTS LT AND RT.

LT and RT may be added to stems by lengthening the L and the R hooks,thus:

tealt.tailt,talt.    tawlt,toalt,toolt.    tielt,toilt.toult.

tilt,telt.talt.    tawlt.tult.toolt.

## INITIAL AND FINAL SL AND SR.

Turn the L hook on the opposite side of the stem from

S circle to represent the double consonant SL,thus:

tisl.tesl.tasl.    tawsl,tusl,toosl.

teasr,taisr,tasr.    tawsr,toasr,toosr.    tiesr,toisr,tousr.

dilt,delt,dalt.    dawlt,dult,doolt.

teald,taild,tald.    tawld,toald,toold.    tield,toild,tould.

teart,tairt,tart.    tawrt,toart,toort,    tiert,toirt,towrt.

## THE FINAL CONSONANTS MT AND NT.

The same principle may be carried out in regard to the initial and final N and M.

teant,taint,tant.    tawnt,toant,toont.    tient,toint,tount.

tind,tend.tand.    tawnd,tund,toond.

stete,state.stat.    stawt,stote,stoot.    stite,stoit,stout.

teamd,taimd,tamd.    tawmd,toamd,toomd.    timed,toimd,tound.

timt,temt,tamt.    tomt,tumt,toomt.

## INITIAL AND FINAL TH AND SH.

TH,initial and final,is represented by a short,curved stem,thus:

theat,thait,that.    thawt,thoat,thoot.    thiet,thoit,thout.

deeth,daith,dath.    dawth,doath,dooth.    dieth,doith,douth.

SH,initial and final,is represented by a small oval loop written upward along the stem,thus:

teash,taish,tash.    tawsh,toash,toosh.    tiesh.toish,toush.

shead,shaid,shad.    shawd,shoad,shood.    shied,shoid,shoud.

The CH and the J stem may be joined to the T stem by writing the T stem upward for the first group,and downward for the second group,thus:

teach,taich,tach.    toch,toach,tooch.    tiech,toich,touch.

## THE FINAL SYLLABLE TION AND SION.

The final syllable TION is added to words by a large oval loop; thus:

tetion,taition,tation.    tawtion,toation,tootion.    etc.

dishen,deshen,dashen.    dawshen,dushen,dooshen.

## INITIAL SN AND SM.

Initial SN and SM are represented by beginning the N and the M circle with a small hook; thus:

snead,snaid,snad.    snawd,snoad,snood.    snied,snoid,snoud.

2

smit,smet,smat.   smot,smut,smoot.

*(shorthand characters)*

Final T or D may be added by extending the SH loop across the stem,the TH curve may be shaded slightly at the end.

dished,dashed,touched,ditched,toothed,tithed.

*(shorthand characters)*

## RE AND LE.

When the initial hooks R and L are lengthened slightly they are pronounced RE and LE.

### READING AND WRITING EXERCISE.

Taste,toast,test,tossed,teased,dazed,dust,deuced,dozed, state,stout,steed,stayed,stead,stud,stood,taster,toaster,tester,duster,tilt,dealt,dolt,tooled,toiled,doled,tart,tort,dwdared,tarred,tired,dowered,taint,taunt,tuned,tint,tent,deigned dined,downed,tanned,tend,teeth,tithe,death,dost,that,thought, dash,sheet,shad,shed,shade,shied,shout,shut,shoot,station, shoots,shudder,shutter,donned,dint,dent,don't,dosed,shouter, stouter,stutter,nettled,muddled,muttered,mattered,mitered, maddened,latent,soddered,shatter,shuddered,rattled,riddled, shattered,teemed,tamed,doomed,timed,tempt,dimmed,dumpt,tender,tempter,dish,dished,doth,doeth,needest,neatest,snood, snide,smitest,smitten,smote,smut,smot,snoot,snout,toothed, tithed,dashed,ditch,touch,teach,stately,retail,retain,rotation,redeem,reduced.

*(shorthand characters)*

NOTE.- In writing the sentences,the pupil should use the shorthand and not the translation,as his guide,and should follow the copy closely,so as to give the characters their proper lengths.   The sentences should be copied carefully at least twenty times.

It was a day of dust and dirt in the town of smut and
'soot. Do not touch the dish. The dish was dashed to atoms.
The attempt was made in the middle of the night. The light
in the middle of the town was dimmed. It was a tool of death.
Death smote the town. The lad rode down in the teeth of the
storm. The dolt stole the dimes. The lad might shut the door
The tired lad shuddered and stared. The dazed writer donned
the duster. The shouter stuttered and smote the tempter.
Don't shatter the dishes. The road was    light. The   towns
are light at night. The muddled dolt deigned to dine down at
the tent. Don't attempt to teach the leader. Don't touch the
letter. Teach the lad to write a letter. State the matter to
the teacher. The neat maid still stood in the door. The lad
tossed the tool to the leader,and turned to shut the shutter.
It is time to start the meeting. The little reader was shut-
out in the storm. The tired steed stood still in the  road
to the little town. The stout dame doled out the tarts to the
little maids. The tired team toiled till night set in.  It
was a sad tale told at the door of the tower. The letter was
torn in the dim light of the store. Don't tempt the lad to
steal the tart. Ten days is the time set for loading the dirt
at the slide.

# CHAPTER VI

## THE CONSONANTS P AND B.

The consonant P is represented by a verticle stem of the same three lengths as the T and the D, differing only in the direction of the writing. Care should be taken not to slant the stem to the left so as to conflict with the T stem.

The consonant B differs from its cognate P only in being slented slightly to the right.

Both the P and the B take the same initials and finals as the T and the D.

Pe,pa,pah.   paw,poe,poo.   pie,poi,pou.

Be.

Pese.

Beest.

Beestr.

Beestes.

Bele.

Pele.

Pere.

Bene.

Pin.

Bemes.

Pills.

Peald.

Peerd.

| Peent. |
| Pitch. |
| Beemd. |
| Bint. |
| Beeth. |
| Bish. |
| Petion. |
| Bitioned. |
| Spe. |
| Spese. |
| Spere. |
| Spins. |
| Spilt. |
| Steep. |
| Snip. |
| Smebe. |
| Thebe. |
| Shepe. |
| Peerst. |
| Epe. |
| Sepe. |
| Eabt. |
| Sips. |
| Lepe. |
| Leaper. |
| Lib. |

Repe.

Rippel.

Reaper.

Nipper.

Mepe.

Pinning.

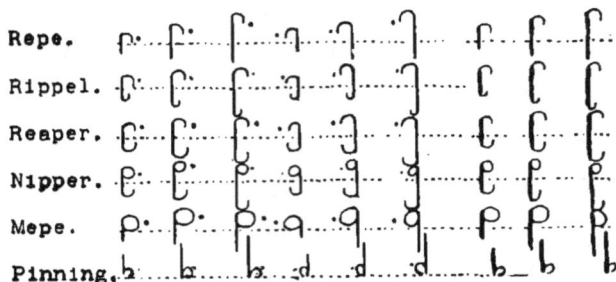

NOTE.--In words of one syllable composed of two stems,
both stems must be the same length and group,so as to represent a continuation of the same sound.

When two stems of the same length are joined together,the
vowel in the second stem is transposed to the beginning of the
stem and the word is spelled phonetically be-ete bete,ba-ate
bate,etc.

D or T before P or B is always written upward.

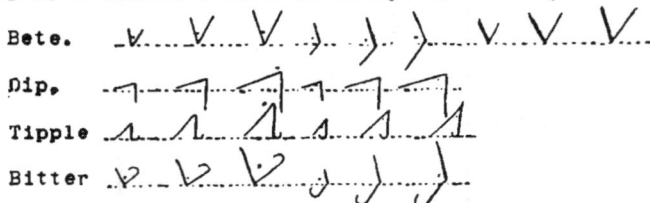

Bete.

Dip.

Tipple

Bitter

D or T following B or P is usually written upward in the
first and the third group,and downward in the second group.

When the M and the N circle begin a stem not across the
line,the M circle is usually pronounced IM,and the N circle,IN

READING AND WRITING EXERCISE.

CAUTION.-- In words of two stems,the side on which the
final hook is turned determines the group to which the word be
longs.

Pay,paw,pooh,pie,spay,spy,peace,pace,pass,passes,pause,
poise,pies,paste,past,paused,pest,post,spies,spiced,spaced,pas-
tor,poster,pester,peal,pale,paley,pall,pole,poley,pool,pile,
pill,pillow,bell,billy,spool,spill,spell,spills,spells,spoils,
spear,spar,spire,spears,spars,spires,spoon,span,spawn,spun,
pierce,pills,pulse,pulls,pools,ape,up,seap,sap,sop,soap,soup,
sip,sup,sips,saps,apes,apple,soaps,slip,sapper,supper,polish,
paying,spying,sipping,slipping,stopping,stepping,punning,pain-
ing,spinning,pining,passing,bossing,poising,parry,bury,sparrow
slop,suppers,steep,stop,stoop,step,steeper,stopper,steeples,
staples,leap,lap,lope,lip,lop,loop,lips,laps,reap,rape,rope,

rap,rip,ripe,ropes,ripple,open,nip,nips,naps,nipper,nippers,
map,slope,mop,mope,bee,bay,bow,by,boy,bough,bees,bays,bass,
toys,boughs,buzz,beast,slap,based,boast,boost,best,bale,bell,
boil,bill,bell,bawl,bean,bane,ban,bon,bone,boon,been,bun,beam
balm,boom,sob,sup,lobe,able,sable,label,labor,labors,lubbers,
robe,rob,rib,rub,slippers,ribbon,robin,nab,knob,nubbin,nibble
mob,slobber,stab,stub,stubble,bases,bosses,puff,buff,bung,pan,
bald,poured,port,pooled,polled,piled,boiled,built,build,bold,
paired,part,bared,bored,pinned,pined,point,pint,pound,bind,
spooned,pines,beams,bones,pins,pans,bounced,spins,sheep,sheep-
ish,shape,shop,push,potion,passion,patience,patient,portion,
path,bath,both,booth,special,bush,species,steepish,snob,
snip,snap,snub,snipe,beamed,boomed,bend,pained,pond,pent,born
bourne,barn,burnt,burst,beard,peerd,pard,bushes,shipper,sleep-
erpalaces,leopard,berth,liable,appoint,partial,stabled,ballast
beat,bate,bat,bought,boat,boot,bite,bitter,better,batter,but -
ter,bitten,button,bottle,bid,bad,bode,buds,bottom,dip,deep,
dipper,dapper,tip,tape,tap,top,type,tipple,topple,obtain,dib-
ble,dabble,speed,spade,spit,spat,spatter,sputter,sputtered,
spattered,spout.

NOTE-- Analyzing and writing the words in each exercise
four or five times from beginning to end will suffice to impress the principles upon the mind sufficiently,but the senten-,
ces should be copied not fewer than ten to twenty times.

Pale stars test dim sight.  Pine poles' suit spears.  The
latest peace matters pester the spies.  Power might pass la-
ter.Paste posters in the shops.  Spears and spars are not made
of tin. The day passes and the time passes.  Toward night the
pole was burned.  The pole was tall.  The rat was a pest to
the pastor.  The pole was made in two pieces.  The maid was
still pale.  The pie was stale,  A lad might pull the pin.
Pain leads to.tears.  Late suppers steal time.  Eat ripe apples.  Pastors pass open store doors. , Step down stairs to supper.  A loop in the rope was made.  A bee stung the snob.  A
pole and a post are in the pool.  An ape ate the soup made of
meet.  A little lad ate the apple.  A knot was in the rope-
ladder.  Boys leap ropes.  Boys eat ripe apples.  Rats nibble
bones.  Robbers rob stores.  Sable robes suit pastors.  Mobs
buy red ribbons.  Boys boom base ball.  The best ball was
made of rubber.  The ribbon was red.  A robin sat in the road.
The boys are not in town.  The boaster made a boast of the matter.  The little maid might spoil the doll.  Both shops are
still open.  The robbers are in the path.  The boys pushed the
matter to test it.  The little boy was in a passion.  The to-
per tippled at the bar.  The butter was bitter and stale.  The
battle of the bosses was bitter.  The boat was at the bottom
of the deep pool.  The bushes are budding.  The boy was bit-
ten by the leopard.  At the tap of the bell the sleeper stood
up.  The bottle slipped down the steep slope.  The beedle
stole the boodle.  The boys battered the barn-door.  The door
at the top of the battered tower was open,and the tall staff
was pulled down off the pulley.  The stuff at the bottom of
the bottle was bitter to the taste.  The double doors stood
open,and the band passed in.  The button was pitched to the
bottom of the stairs.  At the bottom of the dell the road
turns to the right,and stops at the steep slope.  The piston-
was beaten into shape at the shops in Boston.  The beast was
stung by a beetle.  A stunning report was made.

NOTE.-- Speed is often gained by writing the T and the D
stem upward.  In such cases the reversal of the stem causes
the hooks to be reverses and to come on the opposite side of
the stem,thus:

better,butter.door,done,laid,raid,read.

For speed,the R and theL hook initial,on stems of the
third group,are usually written on the left side of the stems,
thus:

write,light,riper,lighter,writer,lightning.

# CHAPTER VII

## THE CONSONANT STEMS K AND GHA.

The consonant K is represented by a straight horizontal
stem of three different lengths, having the same initial and
final circles and hooks as the stems T and D.   The dot above
the stem shows it to be of the First Group; under it, the Second Group.

G (pronounced gay), the cognate of K, differs from K only
in the direction of the writing, the former being slanted downward slightly.

G (gay) in shorthand always has the hard sound, as in
GAME.

ke,ka,kah,  kaw,koe,koo.   kie,koi,kou.

Ske.

Keses.

Keast.

Kister.

Kele.

Kene.

Keme.

Keres.

Skim.

Eke.

Ekel.

Leke.

Lik.

Rik.

Nik.

Kif.

Mik.

Likker.

Ghe.

Gese.

Gele.

Gere.

Geen.

Geems.

League.

Eegs.

Reag.

Gil.

Keart.

Keend.

Geared

Geand.

Keelt.

Gith.

Thick.

Gish.

Shik.

Ketion.

Keech.

Stig.

Nig.

Snig.

Smik.

Tik.

Kepe.

Kit.

Peke.

CAUTION .-- Do not forget the fact that the dot at the be,
ginning of a stem indicates that the vowel in the stem precedes the consonant.

### EXERCISE.

Key,caw,coo,coy,scow,keys,case,cows,kiss,cast,cost,
caused,coast,coaster,keel,call,coal,cool,kill,coil,cull,kin,
ken,came,calm,comb,cares,scheme,skim,scum,scaly,school,scare,
scar,score,scour,skein,scan,cases,causes,eke,ache,oek,aches,
ax,ox,leak,lake,lock,like,lick,luck,look,reek,rake,rock,nick,
knack,knock,nook,meek,make,mock,muck,acres,rockers,liquor,
knuckles,nickel,gay,go,geese,gaze,gas,gauze,gully,golly,goes,
guess,gale,gaily,gall,guy,goose,goal,ghoul,guile,geer,gore,
gain,gory,gone,gun,geme,gum,gills,goals,eggs,leg,lag,log,lug,
league,rig,rag,rug,rogue,gasses,guesses,nag,mug,killed,called,
cold,gold,gilt,callow,carry,curry,culled,card,cared,goured,
canned,gained,cash,gash,shake,shook,caution,scared,scored,
scoured,skinned,scowled,scold,skimmed,scanned,thick,thug,kith,
gush,skiff,skuff,cuff,cough,scoffed,calf,king,gong,geng,re-
gale,current,account,occasion,occurred,cask,regard,record,
slick,slack,sluggishly,sluggard,slag,tick,tickle,tackle,talk
tuck,took,duck,keep,cape,caper,copper,skipper,cod,code,pack,
packer,pickle,pig,pug,poke,back,bag,bog,bug,book,could,cat,
caught,coat.kitten,cotton,cutter,pick,digger,dog,dug,gate,
goat,good,guide,goad,baker,backer,got,scatter,cobble,again,
skimming,looking,leaking,picking,talking,digging,gunning,
scheming,scanning,cunning,coming,causing,kissing,guessing,
gaining.

*[shorthand notation — several lines of handwritten shorthand symbols]*

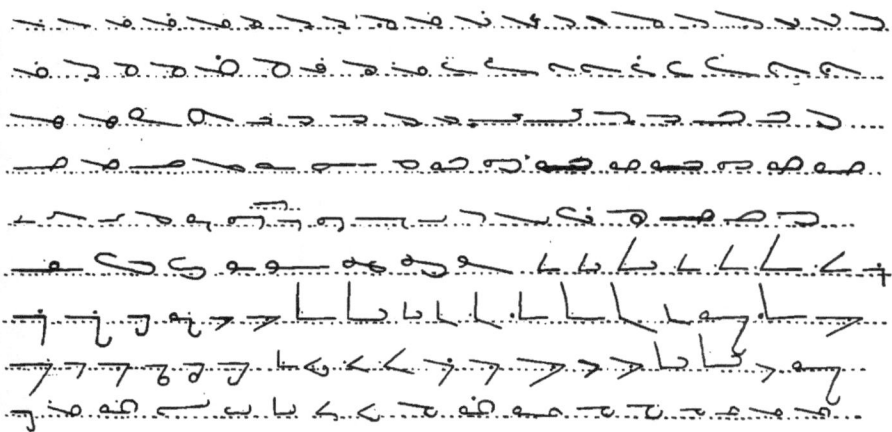

NOTE. -- In words composed of two stems, the group to which the word belongs is determined by the position of the final hook or circle.

Cares can come. Bells can peal. Mobs can rob nobles. Beasts kill bees. Coal pools scare scores. School-boys scale steeples. Robbers' schemes kill noble labor. Scowls scare little boys at school. Schemes are not scarce in times of peace. A score of causes caused the boaster to boast. Coins are made of metal. Boasters lack power. Liquors make wrecks. Lock-makers make locks. Boys tease bees. Oaken doors look neat. Might makes right. Luck makes leaders. Pale boys look meek. An open door was in sight. Tools are made of steel. The dame might buy an acre of coal. Geese like lakes. Calm days came again. Time passes. Guns kill game. Rogues tell tales. Gales come down. Nags go past. Rags make rugs. Boys go to school. Robbers are in the store of the neighbor. The schemes of the robbers came to naught. The boy can tell the tale to the neighbor in town. The sluggard does not dig the garden. The skipper bought a peck of pickles. The rogue stole the copper kettle. The skipper took a bag of copper in the boat. The boy despised the poor topper The skipper ate a ripe red apple at the table. The neighbor paid double toll at the gate. The keeper bought the copper, and beat it into shape. The mob of boys scattered at the tap of the gong. The polite boy despised the rogue. The smoke of the town killed the game. The speaker spoke to the mob.

The liquor in the copper kettle boils.    Good times came again.
The sting of the bee caused the pain.

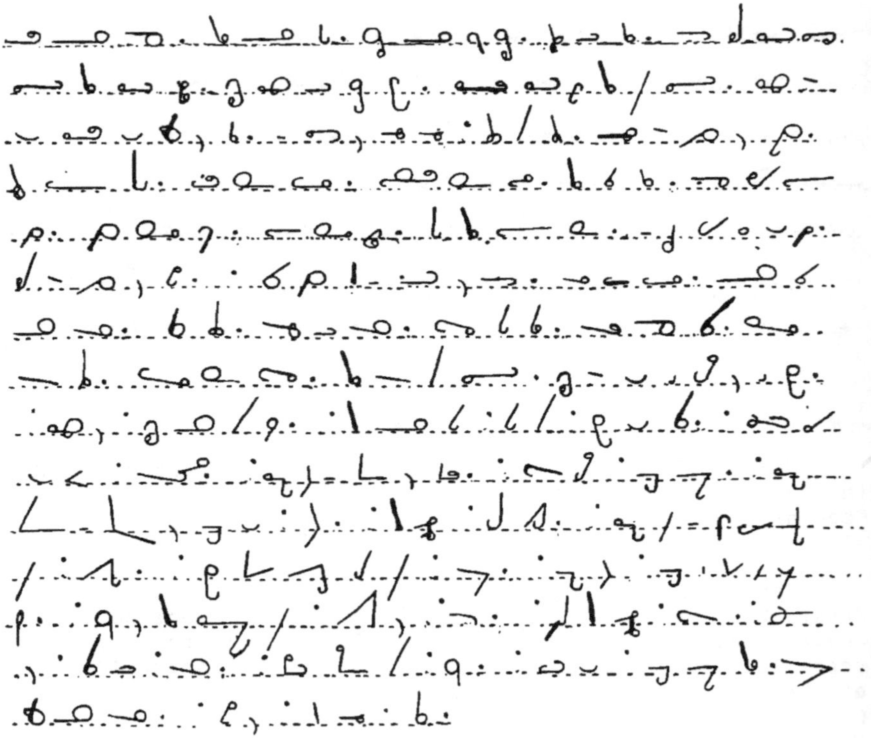

[shorthand text — untranscribable symbols spanning multiple lines]

## EXERCISE.

### Words Composed of Stems of Different Lengths.

NOTE.-- In words of two or more syllables, each stem should be of the proper length to express the exact sound of the syllable it is intended to represent.  It is only the first stem that has its vowel transposed by being written across the line, the other stems being joined to the first without regard to position.

Depart, debar, booty, party, palter, border, pecan, began, begun, became, become, pulpit, builder, scattered, cattle, epic, epitaph, edict, opportune, cabal, cooper, captain, captive, deport, dic-

tation,Duquesne,dapper,turkey,candor,camper,abide,abrupt,ac-
tive,addict,aggregation,appendix,appertain,attic,backbone,bail
bond,bandy,banter,bargain,barricade,barter,base-ball,batting,
beadle,beaker,barn-door,becalm,beguile,beside,bespatter,beto-
ken,betook,binder,bolster,caboose,calico,caliber,campaign,can-
dy,cannibal,carbonic,catarrh,castigation,casting,guitar,coat,
coating,collapse,cordage,correspond,disappoint,county,countess
cowardice,obstacle,abstain,cuspador,dispel,deter,disport,dis-
dain,Boston,piston,garden,recall,regale,repel,repeal,repeat,
rebuff,record,regard,retire,recoil,racket,courteous,gabble,
cobble-stone,tea-kettle,rapid,robust,carpenter ,benediction,
obligation,report,despair,detour,disburse,dispense,despatch,
potato,tobacco,superintend,possible,upholstery,import,impart,
induce, purposely ,legation,characteristic,reptile,reduced,
beginning.

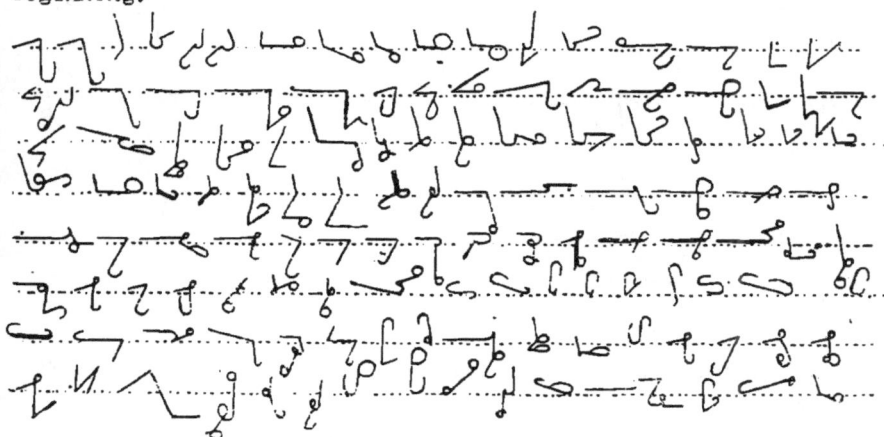

The decay of the party began in the attempt to dictate
terms. The dapper dandy was guilty of cowardice. The captive
had the backbone to banter the captain. Carbonic gas is not
good for a case of catarrh. The ship was becalmed in the Bay
of Biscay. At the banter of the better the bid was taken.
The nag cantered up the county road. The turkey was shot and
killed by the captain of the boat. The bat is in the keeping
of the band. The campers camped at the barricade. The smoke
of the burning barn beguiled the scattered cattle. The pulpit
was bought at a bargain by the party. The painter gave the
barn a coat of red paint. The collapse of the party was due
to an aggregation of causes. The temper of the steel cannot
be depended upon. At an opportune time the report was des-
patched. Possibly the report might be disappointing to the
corresponding parties. In regard to the battle of the cam-
paign,the retired captain called down the robust toaster at
the beginning. The cars are going at rapid speed. A reptile
in the shape of liquor is in the open caboose. It is the duty
of the recorder to write the record in the Gazette,but not to
record it in the book. Night lets the curtain down.

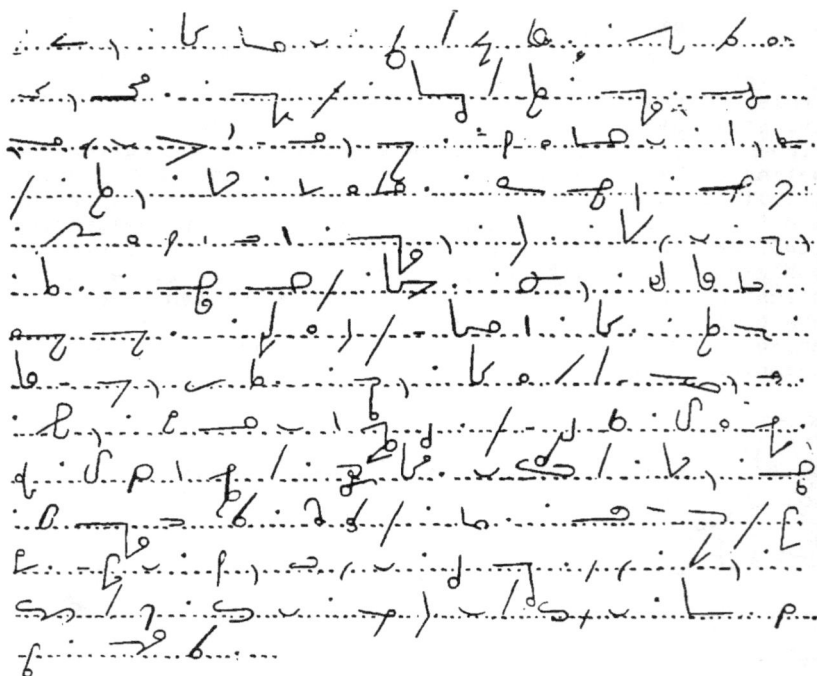

The initial R and L hooks, when lengthened, are pronounced RE end LE.

# CHAPTER VIII.

## THE CONSONANT STEMS F AND V.

The consonant F is represented by a vertical curved stem
The consonant V is similar to the F, but slanting a little to
the right. All curved stems take the circles and hooks on the
concave side.

fee,fay,fay.  faw,foe,foo.  fie,foi,fou.

vee,vey,vah.  vew,voe,voo.  vie,voi,vou.

efe,afe,af.  awf,ofe,oof.  ife,oif,ouf.

if,ef,af.  of,uf,oof.

seve,save,sav.  sov,sove,soov.  sive,soiv,souv.

fese,fase,fas.  fos,fose,foos.  fise,fois,fous.

fis,fes,fas.  fos,fus,foos.

lefe,lafe,laf.  lof,loaf,loof.  life,loif,louf.

vele,vale,val.  vol,vole,vool.  vile,voil,voul.

vil,vel,val.  vol,vul,vool.

3

refe,rafe,raf.  rof,rofe,roof.  rife,roif,rouf.

rif,ref,raf.  rof,ruf,roof.

vere,vare,var.  vor,vore,voor.  vire,voir,vour.

reme,fame,fam.  fom,fome,foom.  fime,foim,foum.

kefe,kafe,kaf.  kof,kofe,koof.  kife,koif,kouf.

fin,fen,fan.  fon,fun,foon.

vene,vane,van.  'von,vone,voon.  vine,voin,voun.

fish,fesh,fash.  fosh,fush,foosh.

shefe,shafe,shaf.  shof,shofe,shoof.  shife,shoif,shouf.

feath,faith,fath.  foth,foath,footh.  fieth,foith,fouth.

theif,thaif,thaf.  thof,thoaf,thoof.  thief,thoif,thouf.

fib,feb,fab.  fob,fub,foob.

deaf,daif,daf.  dof,doef,doof.  dief,doif,douf.

NOTE.-- The stems T and D are usually written upward when followed by the stems F or V.

The aspirate H is indicated by a short tick across a stem, at the beginning for the first group, and at the end for the second group. The shaded tick represents the long sound the light tick the short sound. *

fete,fate,fat.     fot,fote,foot.     fite,foit,fout.

veke,vake,vak.     vok,voak,vook.     vike,voik,vouk.

NOTE.-- If the third stem of the Second Group is shaded slightly at the end, it takes the sound of U instead of OO.

When the curve in a stem is almost a semi-circle it has the same effect as if the stem were written across the line; that is, the vowel comes first.

## READING AND WRITING EXERCISE.

Fee,foe,fie,vie,evil,if,of,eve,awful,face,foes,loaf,vice, leaf,few,fewer,view,voice,vows,leaves,lave,laugh,lives,feel, fall,fill,fell,fail,fool,file,folly,fowl,veal,vole,rife,rifle, raffle,safer,cipher,vital,voter,feeder,fiddle,deceiver,deceive,cave,cough,skiff,effect,fog,fig,fury,firey,vogue,pave, puff,river,rover,fierce,force,farce,rafter,rueful,cuffy,filly over,foil,sphere,forests,gulf,curve,careful,carve,devout,defeat,terrific,fender,defender,discover,deliver,definite,testify,develop,feigning,fan,fun,finder,fainter,founder,fatal,fatten,faltering,faker,fishes,faith,faithful,even,paver,beaver, peevish,beefish,foolish,before,befall,befell,defaming,difficulty,deficit,deficient,fife,festive,votive,laughing,loving, fitting,recovering,pacific,benefit,beneficial,specific,venture feature,opportunity,foresight,defined,lawfully,filtered,defer. refer,effective,telephone,officially,dividend,revising,different,defiant,fulfilled,forcible,form,reform,perversions,devotion,bereft,bereave,ventilate,feeling,fearing,failing,falling, vividly,haversack,heavily,hove,hovering,revealed,vanity,forestall,perfectly,supervisor,deference,deferred,referred.

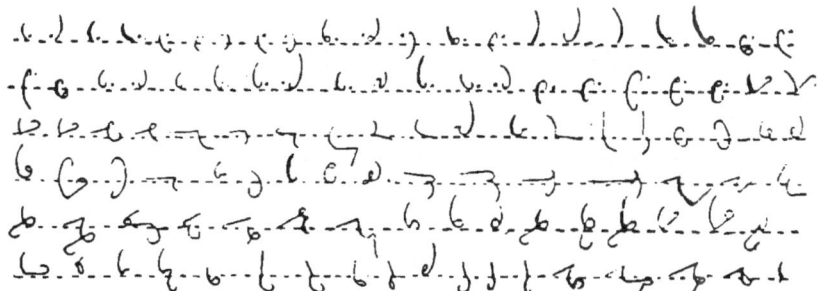

The fierce rover fell off the roof of his stockade. The
tale of the deceiver deceived the careful defender of the cave
Can the finder testify to the false tale? The boy tells a
definite tale of his defeat. A safer road can be found by
the forest. Be careful, boys at the curve of the road, to look
for the cars. Be careful to vote right at the polls. Be
ever faithful to the duty. The lads roved off into the forest.
The thieves made off, laid the gold, and stowed it in the ship.
The rovers shoved the boat into the bay. The thief rowed over
the river in a boat. The bad boys stole the boat, and rowed it
over the river. The lad is deficient in his upper sphere.
The knave fell into the awful gulf. The fish are in the river.
The event came off at the time set for it. Often times the
boy became sad. A boy ate a biscuit and a potato. The deceiver met a terrible obstacle. The ship stuck fast and was pulled off the snag. The thief fell into the river before the
boats. The boy might make an effort to obtain the gift. The
effort was after his full approval. The bill of lading was
laid upon the bookkeeper's desk. The table was covered by
coins. The party happened to go his road.

# CHAPTER IX

## THE CONSONANTS CH AND J.

The double consonants CH and J are represented by straight stems written downward similar to the T and the D stems, but having a distinct shading at the lower end; thus:

che, chay, chah.   chaw, choe, choo.   chie, choi, chou.

je, jay, jah.   jaw, joe, joo.   jie, joi, jou.

each, aitch, atch.   otcn, oatch, ootch.   ietch, oitch, outch.

eje, aje, aj.   oj, oaj, ooj.   ᵛije, oij, ouj.

Re-write the lines above, giving the stems the short vowel sounds.

seje, saje, saj.   soj, soaj, sooj.   sije, soij, souj.

leach, laich, lach.   loch, loach, looch.   liech, loich, louch.

reach, raich, rach.   roch, roach, rooch.   riech, roich, rouch.

cheer, chere, char.   chor, chore, choor.   chire, choir, chour.

fitch, fetch, fatch.   fotch, futch, footch.

jene, jane, jan.   jon, jone, joon.   jine, join, joun.

jeke,jake,jak. jok,joke,jook. jike,joik,jouk.

chit,chet,chet. chot,chut,choot.

cheard,chaird,cherd. cnerd,choard,choord. etc.

jilt,jelt,jalt. jolt,jult,joolt.

jim,jem,jam. jom,jum,joom.

neje,naje,naj. noj,noje,nooj. nije,noij,nouj.

thitch,thetch,thatch. thotch,thutch,thootch.

jele,jele,jal. jol,jole,jool. jile,joil,joul.

chist,chest,chast. chost,chust,choost.

chaf,chef,chaf. chof,chuf,choof.

chint,chent,chant. chont,chunt,choont.

## READING AND WRITING EXERCISE.

Chew,jew,each,jaw,edge,seige,sage,hedge,such,notch,nitch,
hitch,match,major,much,chop,chuck,joke,jib,cheat,jade,cheek,
choke,teach,touch,chalk,ditch,Dutch,peach,patch,cage,chin,gin,
jam,cheer,fetch,chief,gentle,chuckle,chaff,jove,ravage,package
leakage,chieftain,cottage,object,subject,gentile,jumble,kitch-
en,richly,jump,negligence,courage,hatch,chilly,gill,choose,
just,chest,jester,cudgel,vigil,agile,satchel,jolly,chamber,

midget,budget,thatch,chant,chester,leach,latch,jabber,jobber,
chain,jammed,reach,roach,ratchet,jumper,lodge,chilled,jilt,ob-
jection,reject,legislator,legend,legendary,passage,jolting,edg
ing,adjusted, coinage ,purchase,apologist,justly,Egypt,foliage
voyage,suffrage,forgery,corrupt,skeleton,repetition,distil,em-
balmed,deposit,upholstery,temperate,abolish,spectacle,candle,
kinder,superstitious,redeemable,disappoint,stumble,hovering,

NOTE--The final M circle shaded takes the sound of MP.

Camp,pump,pomp,scamp,dump,damp,scimp,pimp,tamp,decamp,
stemp,compass,bump,gimp,encamp,vamp,chump,jump,champ.

assist a neighbor if possible. The pastor left a package
at the store. State the object of the cipher. The joker ate
the peaches of the chief. Savage dogs bark at night. The
boy laughed at the jumper. The poor slave locked the door of
the chamber. The agile savage pitched the package to the
chieftain. The sage touched the pole. The ball lodged in
the thatched roof. The little girl jumped the rope. The jumper can jump over the deep ditch. The fox caught the goose by
the neck. The dog was choked by a bone. The little girl
reached for the spoon. The charred piece of timber fell into
the river. The jolt made the box fall. The thug looks meek
to-day. Birds eat seeds. The noble was at the bath. The
booth was opened by the boys. The rogue stole the liquor. At
the time spoken of,it was impossible. The party became sober.

An apology was justly due the temperate speaker. The faithful pastor labored diligently to prevent the disappointing
spectacle.

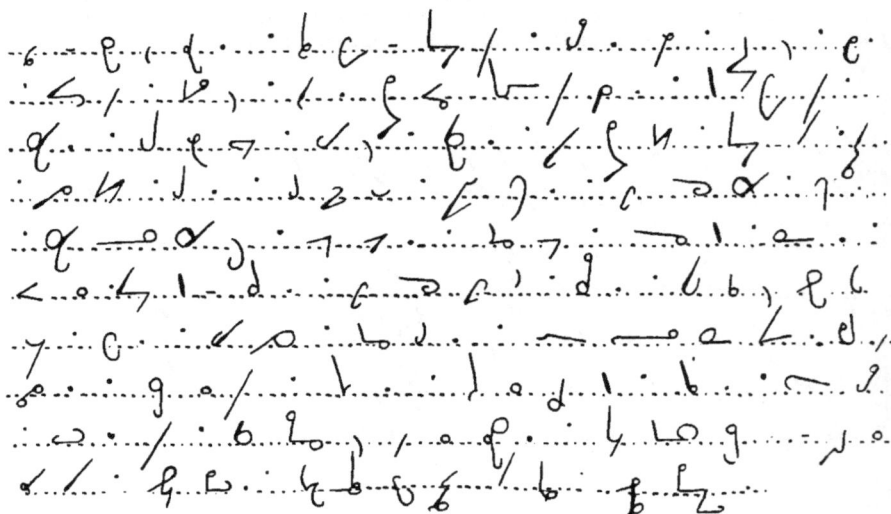

CH and J,initial and final.are represented by a shaded
hook,thus:

judge,touch,teach,ditch,chief,chewed.catch,coach.

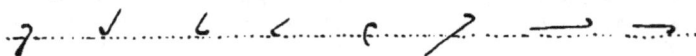

# CHAPTER X.

## THE CONSONANT STEMS S AND Z.

The consonant S is represented by a curved stem slanting to the left. Z is represented by a stem with a still greater slant to the left.

se,say,sah.　saw,soe,soo.　sie,soi,sou.

sese,sase,sas.　sos,soas,soos.　sies,sois,sous.

lese,lese,las.　los,loes,loos.　lise,lois,lous.

rese,rese,ras.　ros,roas,roos.　rise,rois,rous.

sele,sele,sal.　sol,soal,sool.　sile,soil,soul.

sere,sare,sar.　sor,soar,soor.　sire,soir,sour.

seme,seme,sam.　som,some,soom.　sime,soim,s oum.

seke,sake,sak.　sok,soke,sook.　sike,soik,souk.

sint,sent,sant.　sont,sunt,soont.

seald,saild,sald.　sold,soald,soold.　sield,soild,sould.

zele,zale,zol.　zol,zole,zool.　zile,zoil,zoul.

eze,aze,az.　oz,oze,ooz.　ize,oiz,ouz.

seeth,saith,sath.　soth,soath,sooth.　sithe,soith,south.

seash,seish,sash.　sosh,soash,soosh.　sishe,soish,soush.

sission,session,sassion.　sossion,sussion,soossion.

## READING AND WRITING EXERCISE.

See,say,saw,so,sue,sign,ease,ace,ooze,is,ceased,size,hiss
lease,lace,loose,lose,race,rice,rouse,seal,sale,soul,soil,
silly,sell,sour,sore,soak,sack,city,tussle,sicker,castle,ask,
busy,cozy,baser,haze,chisel,jostle,silk,silky,search,service,
survey,rustle,wrestle,razor,racer,escape,soiled,sold,seldom,
seared,sword,sired,soured,signed,hose,sound,sounder,centre,
saunter,seem,same,sane,zone,soon,seemed,house,sailed,silken,
silver,diligent,deserve,sung,sulking,seize,rescind,syndicate,
sagacity,fancy,suspend,suspenders,ascertain,design,designing,
position,possession,successful,sustain,suspicion,sincere,as-
sist,serious,south,sympathy,desire,systematic,recently,saintly
persistently,resolute,sulphuric,result,pursuance,received,deci-
sion,officer,reasonable,disaster,solicit,assemblage,assailed,
Genesis,revolver,thousands,facility,December,desolate,stipu-
late,discount,disposed,associate,residue,design,resign,sully,
sing,sang,song,sinning,sunning,signing,sorry,sailing,soaring.

A baser metal can be made of tin.  A careful surveyor
surveyed the soil of the city.  The edge of the chisel is dull
The mob sacked the city at night.  The case of silk fell off
the boat.  The wreck is over the river at the depot.  The ci-
der soured in the vessel.  In the centre was a fine silver tea
service.  The session was soon over, and the door was shut and
locked.  By the aid of the soldier, the vessel was discovered,
and a diligent search was made for the sword.  The coon ate
the tin can of thick soup.  The cautious boy shook the car.
The goose stuck in the mud.  The lad tamed the deer.  The
stag ate the shock of corn.  A lugger came to the coast in
the night.  The slave escaped in a sail-boat.  Slavery was
abolished in the South in 1862.  The bounty was paid over to
the soldier.  The position was not desirable.  Possession was
taken at the point of the bayonet.  In pursuence of the decision of the court, possession was given.

# CHAPTER XI.

## THE CONSONANT STEM W.

The consonant W is represented by a shaded stem slanting upward to the right.

we,way,wah.   waw,woe,woo.   wie,woi,wou.

When the vowel is transposed by writing the W stem through the line,the accent is on the second syllable.

ewe,away,awah.   awaw,awoe,awoo.   awie,awoi,awou.

swe,swa,swah.   swaw,swoe,swoo.   swie,swoi,swou.

wene,wane,wan.   won,wone,woon.   wine,woin,woun.

weer,ware,war.   wor,wore,woor.   wire,woir,wour.

wele,wale,wal.   wol,wole,wool.   wile,woil,woul.

weme,wame,wam.   wom,wome,woom.   wime,woim,woum.

wepe,wape,wap.   wop,wope,woop.   wipe,woip,woup.

wint,went,want.   wont,wunt,woont.

weke,wake,wak.   wok,woke,wook.   wike,woik,wouk.

wilt,welt,walt.    wolt,wult,woolt.

with.weth.wath.    woth,wuth,wooth.

wish,wesh,wash.    wosh,wush,woosh.

wist,west,wast.    wost,wust,woost.

NOTE.-- The M and the N circle at the beginning of stems
are frequently pronounced IM and IN.

READING AND WRITING EXERCISE.

We,way,woe,woo,swan,wine,wane,weep,wife,wait,win,woes.
wit,swoon,week,wake,winter,wonder,waistcoat,wicked,wabble,
awhile,swain,waif,with,swath,swill,swell,swale,swim,swam,
swore,wealth,worth,welsh,welter,warder,wider,western,west,
waste.wistful.watchful.witch.wench,wings.awaiting.stockade.
walking.wakeful,wheel.whale.whack,weakening.willow.wallow.wea-
ry,worry.wooly,willing,winning,twill,twist,dwelling,whistle,

The waistcoat of the waiter was a wonder to the neighbors.
The busy maid searched the kitchen for the whisk.  The waiter
walked over the gulf at night.  The cozy widow patched the
waistcoat for the dirty sweeper of the sidewalk.  A package

of silk was left at the cottage. We awoke at day-light. We
might discover the object of the jest. The wit was scarce
and the wisdom was weak. The careful boy will not lose the
watch. The smack is in the bay. The teeth of the beast are
of bone. The rogue came down to the lake. We wished to obtain the package as soon as it was possible to get it. We ab
stained because we wished to postpone the passage of the bill.
The desperate fool made a disturbance, and we made an attempt
to dampen his temper. We wish to make such a diversion as wil
will stop the cutting of the forests. The weather is colder
to-day. Politics govern the city. We might make an effort to
stem the tide of opposition.

# CHAPTER XII

## THE CONSONANT STEMS M AND N.

The consonant stem M is represented by a curved horizontal stem. The stems of the Second Group are slanted downward slightly to render them more distinct from the First Group.

me,may,moh.    maw,moe,moo.    mie,moi,mou.

NOTE.-- As the horizontal stems are not written across the line to indicate that the vowel comes first,the same fact is indicated by giving the stems a greater curve. The same rule extends to all curved stems,namely,that the transposition of the vowel is indicated by giving a greater curve to the stems.

eme,eme,am.    om,ome,oom.    ime,oim,oum.

im,em,am.    om,um,oom.

The consonant N is represented  by a horizontal stem curved in the opposite direction from the M.

ne,ney,nah.    naw,noe,noo.    nie,noi,nou.

ene,ane,an.    on,one,oon.    ine,oin,oun.

reme,reme,ram.    rom,rome,room.    rime,roim,roum.

mere,mere,mar.    mor,more,moor.    mire,moir,mour.

leme,lame,lam.    lom,lome,loom.    lime,loim,loum.

mele,male,mal.　mol,mole,mool.　mile,moil,moul.

mene,mane,man.　mon,mone,moon.　mine,moin,moun.

nim,mem,mam.　mom,mum,moom.

rene,rane,ran.　ron,rone,roon.　rine,roin,roun.

nene,nane,nan.　non,none,noon.　nine,noin,noun.

lene,lane,lan.　lon,lone,loon.　line,loin,loun.

nim,nem,nam.　nom,num,noom.

nele,nale,nal.　nol,nole,nool.　nile,noil,noul.

milt,melt,malt.　molt,mult,moolt.

nere,nare,nar.　nor,nore,noor.　nire,noir,nour.

mint,ment,mant.　mont,munt,moont.

mith,meth,math.　moth,muth,mooth.

sme,sma,smah.　smaw,smoe,smoo.　smie,smoi,smou.

sne,sna,snah.　snaw,snoe,snoo.　snie,snoi,snou.

mish,mesh,mash.   mosh,mush,moosh.

theme,theme,them   thom,thome,thoom.   thime,thoim,thoum.

shim,shem,sham.   shom,shum,shoom.

mission,mession,massion.   mossion,mussion,moosion.

mist,mest,mast.   most,must,moost.

## READING AND WRITING EXERCISE.

Me,may,maw,my,mow,knee,know,gnaw,new,nigh,nay,now,roam,
ream,rhyme,lame,lime,loom,mare,mar,mere,moon,mire,main,moan,
mine,nose,knees,knows,nice,mice,noise,mouse,mace,roomer,knave
former,foreign,march,amaze,balmy,bony,cony,mazy,noisy,money,
many,amnesty,ounce,lounge,round,funny,china,most,masses,mental
mister,inspire,render,lender,mill,mole,mile,male,mountain,
solemnity,shine,sham,shun,mission,nation,national,notion,mint,
meant,moaned,mind,mound,named,nomination,nominal,theme,them,
than,thin,thinner,thumb,melt,corner,column,balance,mist,nosed
musty,mastiff,range,ranch,stormy,owners,season,vicinity,in-
ducement,assignment,equipment,monopoly,renewal,channel,negoti-
ate,him,ham,hum,hamper,hanker,hone,hunker,moaning,remaining,
motioning,moving ,emotional,nelly,nelly,milly,mellow.appear-
ance,management,financial,enchant,tendency,documents,nobili-
ties,manufacture,unload,injunction,department,locomotion,navi-
gation,unpardonable,remittance,to-morrow,amicable,domestic, '
mechanic,intelligent,indulgent,standard,emphatic,denial,misre-
presentation,accompany,infer,inference,inferred,unlikely,an-
nounced,maintain,passenger,merchandise,materiel,immaterial,mis
taken,invariable,disappoint,undersigned,acknowledge,desponden-
cy, informed,information,enumeration,necessity,necessarily,
necessary,unnecessary,furnish,furniture,undismayed,admission,
admit,unable,inability,occurrence,meantime,memorandum,light-
ning,government,recommend,enjoyment,superintend,maximum,in-
sert,insertion,intoxicating,development,engagement,encourage-
ment,currency,entire,differential,demolished,infidelity,in-
herit,margin,assassination,institutions,reinforced,magnifi-
cence,diminish,penalty,utterance,meteoric,monsters,magnitude,
dishonest,insensible,annuity,damage,namely,manufactory,custo-
mer,'alance,mileage,percentage,immediately,unanswered,manipu-

late,imagination,misapprehend ,annointment,moment,angel,rever
ential, image,imagine,countenence,majesty,minister,mumbling,
column,miscellaneous,destiny,engaged,arranged,steamer,indorse-
ment.

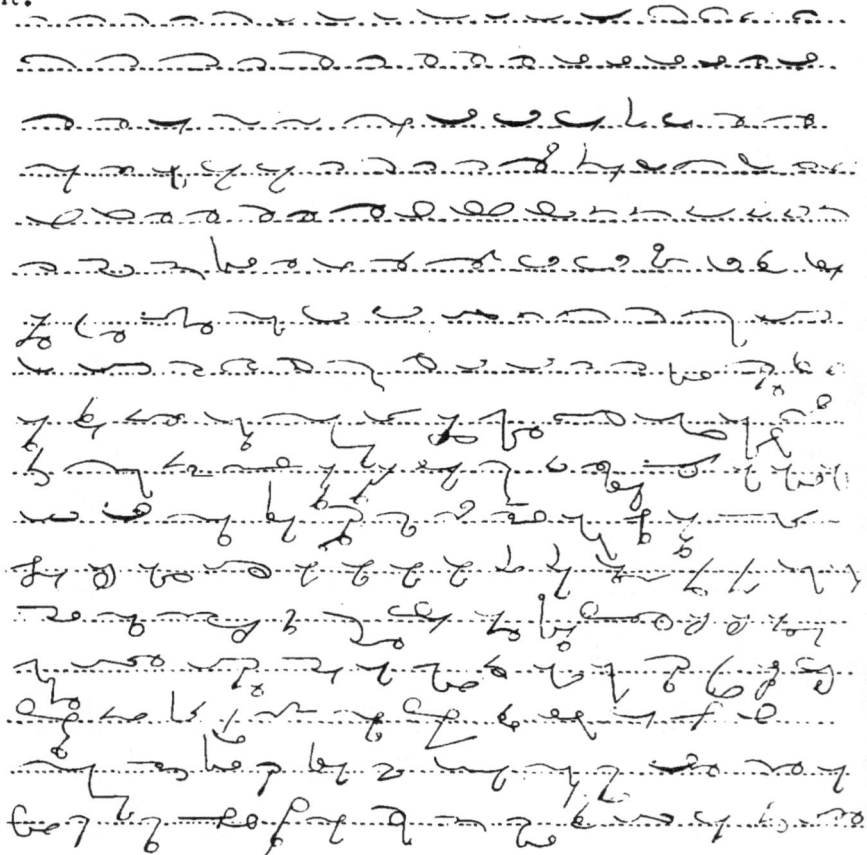

NOTE.-- Slant the M stems of the second group downward
slightly to distinguish them from those of the First Group.

    The balmy winds of March soon take away the snow.    Mice
eat nuts and corn.  Money makes knaves of men.  Some men tell
too much.  My noisy neighbor was a foreigner.  The moon gives
light at night.  Many moons may come and go before we may see
the like again.  We may inspire courage.  We might insist on
amnesty to the masses.  Again we inspire courage to resist
evil.  The moon shown down upon the forest.  We saw the moun:-
tain in the dim distance.  The sare read in the stars the fate
of the nation.  The scared boy staggered down the lane.  The
poor little maid was still and patient.  The new book is thick.

er than it was before. The obligation is such that we cannot
resist the appeal. We made an application for the position.
Fuel was not abundant in the city during the cold weather, but
soon came in rapidly when the snow disappeared. The county at
torney is an officer of the State.

# CHAPTER XIII

## DOUBLE CONSONANTS.

The consonants T,P,K,with their cognates,and F unite with the consonant R to form double consonants,and are indicated by writing the stems a short distance above the line.

tre,tra,trah.　traw,troe,troo.　trie,troi,trou.

bre,bra,brah.　braw,broe,broo.　brie,broi,brou.

kre,kra,krah.　kraw,kroe,kroo.　krie,kroi,krou.

fre,fra,frah.　fraw,froe,froo.　frie,froi,frou.

The consonant V,the cognate of F,will not combine with R to form a double consonant,as vre,vra,vrah,etc.,and therefore the R must come after the vowel;thus:

vere,vare,var.　vor,vore,voor.　vire,voir,vour.

The consonants P,K,F,with their cognates and S unite with L to form double consonants,and are indicated by writing the stems below the line.

ple,pla,plah.　plaw,ploe,ploo　plie,ploi,plou.

gle,gle,glah.　glaw,gloe,gloo　glie,gloi,glou.

fle,fla,flah.　flaw,floe,floo.　flie,floi,flou.

Since V will not unite with L,as vle,vla,vlan,etc.,the L
must follow the vowel; thus:

vele,vale,val.   vol,vole,vool.   vile,voil,voul.

sle,sla,slah.   slaw,sloe,sloo.   slie,sloi, slou.

The S stem under the line forms a double consonant with
L,but placed above the line it will not unite with R,as sre,
sra,srah,etc.,but must be pronounced sere,sare,sar,etc.; thus:

sere,sare,sar.   sor,sore,soor.   sire,soir,sour.

In words composed of two or more stems,it is only the
first stem that combines with R or L by being written above or
below the line.

## EXERCISE.

Tree,blow,tray,blew,true,glee,try,glow,dray,flee,draw,
flay,dry,flaw,pray,flow,craw,flew,crow,fly,fry,slay,grow,sly,
grew,slow,free,flies,fray,flows,dress,fleece,trays,slice,
strays,split,straws,plight,sprays,blood,screwsbleed,freeze,
flaws,frays,floater,trick,glades,clover,track,cleave,trust,
closed,breed,blessed,pressed,imply,impressive,reply,trustful,
incline,refrain,fluster,retrench,reclaim,intrinsic ,implore
profane,clasp,profligate,replete,translate,blockade,transit.
plain,retrieve,flicker,presume,fleck,trouble,fleeter,gruff,
glove,crane,clove,brave,bless,brief,cliff,reproof,clung,im-
prove,glass,grief,class,grove,classify,grave,claim,drink,cla-
mor,drunk,fling,frank,flank,strung,plank,freek,clang,break,
cling,cringe,bluff,greater,cloth,trimmed,clinch,triple,plant
French,Florida,profitable,plunge,prejudicial,plenty,preach,re-
flection,prudently,Cleveland,presume,clerk,presumption,flannel
transmit,slur,transmission,glorify,promote,apply,promotion,
regular,draft,blasphemy,trampling,regulate,preservation,clear-
ness,regret,reclaim,tremendous,clever,scrupulous prolonged,
clash,crash,clam,fraudulent,clew,preference,clay,breweries,
glue,strata,glare,triumphant,ecclesiastical,literal,slim,ap-
prove,slake,transfer,pleasure,pressure,revelation,precious,
clause,sprinkled,flip,traffic,flop,increase,flush,prosper,
flake transpose,flock, precisely  ,plush,transferred,clutch,
preferring,pledge,preference,slain,gravity,gloom,private,
gloaming,principle,flimsy,driven,flame,travel,flag,prior,
flesh,traverse,florist,drench,plain,trench,plaster,streaming,
climax,straining,glinting,cramp,cleaning,grinning,cloudy.

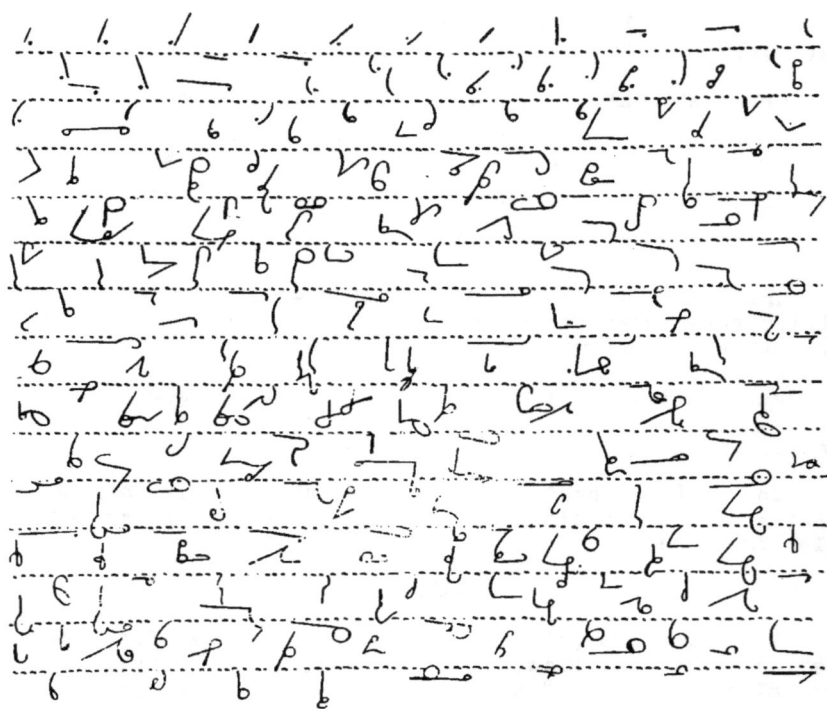

Impressive services took place at the grave of the deceased prisoner of war. We discovered no trace of the stray cattle. The result of the search impressed us by its awful solemnity. We reclaimed a greater part of the soil by a broad and deep drain. We incline to believe the story to be true. The reply was such to inspire trustfulness. Great stress was laid on the fact of his innocence. Upon mature reflection the transaction was transferred to another classification. We regret the impression was not so clear and pleasing as we were inclined to look for. Greater profits were not obtainable at the time the trouble occurred in the camp. The brewery proffered assistance, and it was not accepted. A brief reproof was administered to the noisy class. The precise story of his troubles was precisely true.

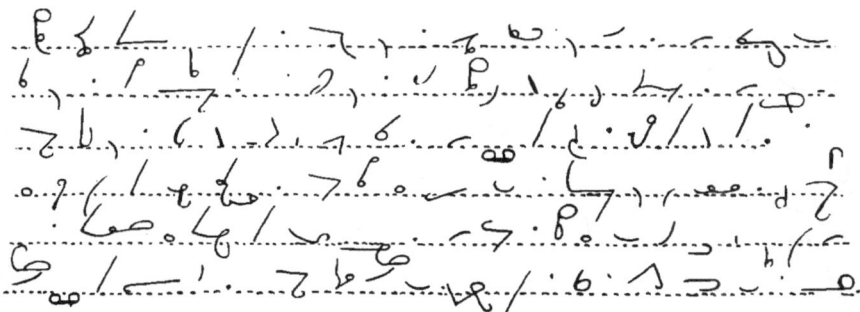

The placing of all other stems including the vowel stems except those stems which unite with R and L to form double consonants, above or below the line, indicates that the stem ends with R or L respectively.

### EXERCISE.

Cheer, chair, char, mere, mar, more, sore, nor, neal, meal, mail, jail, will, well, wail, were, remorse, resource, inward, military, millinery, mouldy, murder, mortal, molten, miracle, remark, sources mercy, knowledge, serve, reserve, mourn, mourner, ceremony, north, nearest, merest, mortgage, milker, surrender, sermon, violate, honorable, energy, enlarge, northern, worth, analysis, enormous, valid, nerve, nervous, milder, reverberations, delay, wilderness, circuit circumstances, multitude, unreasonable, charter, moreover, merit, meritorious, immersed, immersion, surety , surely, only, analyze. dealer. serial. cereal.

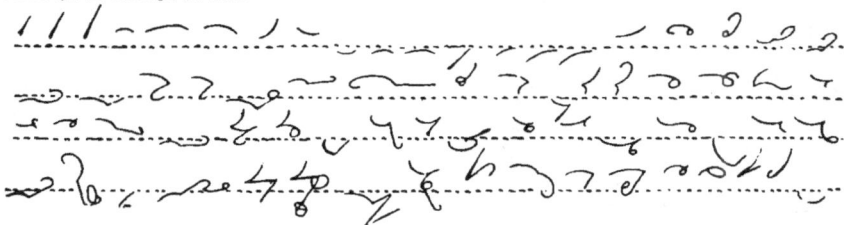

The wicked woman implored the stricken man for mercy. A wail of remorse impressed us as we walked down the gloomy corridoe of the prison. Man is mortal, The right kind of knowledge,is an inward source ofblissin time of trouble. We were stricken with remorse. We were very glad of the honor. The p place of honor was reserved for his parents. The analysis pre sents great impurity. The majority must prevail in the national council. The man with plenty of energy will succeed. The pursuit was abandoned. The struggle was still maintained. The new serial story will give the market price of cereals every week. Immense numbers of Germans came from the North. A few only returned to the forests of the North.

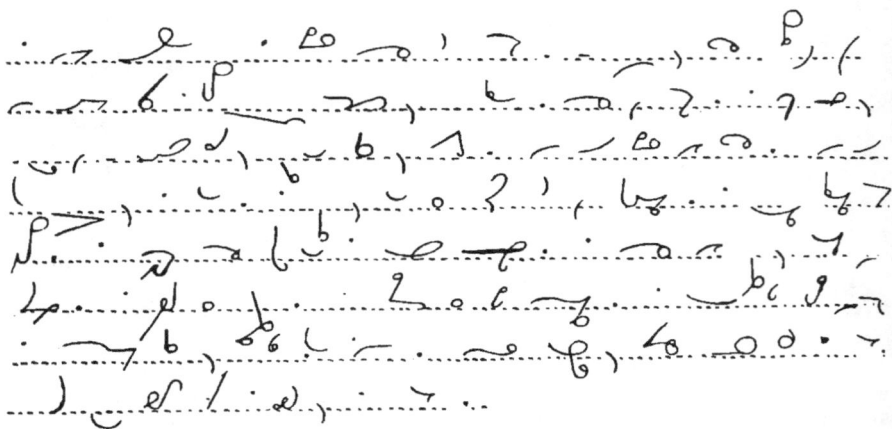

Double consonants may also be indicated by cutting the first stem by the second,for R,and writing the second very close to the first for L,in the following manner:

Telegram,program,telegraph,disagree,degree,fragrant,flagrant,disgrace,inscribe,subscribe,caprice,deprive,progress, digression,preclude,discipline,deplore,decline,superfluous, photographed,nostril,secretary,emigrant,duplicate,prostration, re-inclose,duplicity,children,surplus,engraved,procrestination neutral,Democratic,instrument,demonstration,entrench,instruction,district,distract,destruction,accomplishment.

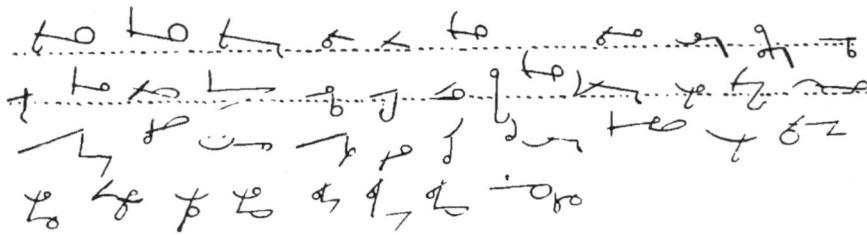

## SENTENCES.

The district attorney prosecuted the criminal. The prostration of the officer precluded all attempts at restoring discipline. The caprice of the scoundrel caused him (im ) to decline the secretary's gracious offer. The frail platform fell with a terrible crash. The unscrupulous politician seemed to deplore the disgraceful result. The fragrant flowers were placed on the pulpit for the minister. The discrepancy proved to be simply a blunder of the clerk's. To him, duty--" stern daughter of the voice of God"--was ever paramount. Slavery was the apple of discord between the North and the South. An obstruction was built in the district road-way.

# CHAPTER XIV.

## PRIMARY VOWELS.

The primary vowels of the language are represented as follows:

e, a, ah.    aw, o, oo.    i, oi, ou.

Each of these stems has two sounds, a long and a short sound. Write the stems, pronouncing each, first with its long, and then with its short sound. Write the E stem upward and the OO stem downward.

CAUTION.-- Remember that the vowel comes first in stems that are curved more than usual.

She, sha, shah.    shaw, sho, shoo.    shi, shoi, shou.

Ish, esh, ash.    osh, ush, oosh.

### EXERCISE.

NOTE.-- A slight shading of a vowel stem at the end, adds T or D. The third group of the SH stem has also the sound of CH in many words.

Eye, ice, iron, ear, eel, A, air, are, ah, ale, all, or, oral, owl, owe, hour, hourly, urn, erred, oil, lie, lay, layer, rare, rarely, island, islander, Ireland, own, ill, oiled, aired, ore, earned, shy, shore, royal, asher, ocean, ash, ooze, shown, omitted, allow, issue, issued, she, show, Erie, aspect, bible, rash, rashly, banishment, punishment, astonishment, rely, shears, shrive, shrine, share, shower, shell, shall, shame, error, shaw, else, elsewhere, orderly, rule, ruler, rural urge, urgently, origin, original, arm, armor, old, older, earl, sharp, shelf, owning, row, early, alarm, ray, ewry, relations, below, pillow, carouse, roar, allay, ally, owed, odd, add, had, hard, order, hardly, heard, aired, chagrin, machine, machinery, artificial, ordinary, heretofore, joy, enjoy, rejoice, enjoin, choice, china, arbitrary.

*[shorthand symbols]*

Our ears are not even open to the truth. Who can tell
all a day or an hour may bring forth. Our share in the ceremony was very brief. Our names were mentioned in the journal
The majority must rule in our land. Strike while the iron is
still hot. The earl is now earning his own living. While the
king was passing the bells were pealing, and the cannon were
booming. Pausing for a moment she saw her error. The homi-
cide was hung. The fruit hangs high in the tree.

*[shorthand symbols]*

## COMBINATIONS OF CONSONANTS.

When the R hook initial on the Second Group side of a
stem is made twice its usual size, it is pronounced RES; thus:

Respect, rescue, restore, response. residue, receipt, restric-
tion.

*[shorthand symbols]*

The R hook final, made twice its usual size is pronounced
either LER or REL; thus:

Pearl, girl, furl, tailor, dealer, federal, mineral, scholar.

*[shorthand symbols]*

# READING AND WRITING EXERCISE.

Carry,marry,narrow,very,bury,merry,story,valley,dealer,
tailor,federal,jailor,mineral,elbow,alone,alphabet,fuller,dul-
ler,alcove,morasses,molasses,alchemist,carelessly,scholar,vic-
tory,victorious,lesson,listen,testamentary,mockery,mystery,to-
morrow,barrow,caress,tallow,gory,emery,notary,dairy,fairy,ob-
serve,ring,rung,settlers,allowance,liberal,erect,corporation,
color,fabulous,actively,barlow,irregular,literal,perusal,elle-
gation,really,responsible,arrive,burly,artillery,hereby,irredi
ate,array,orbit,artistic,supernatural,unroll,interior,super-
ior,hereafter,lower,generally,emperor,allude,allusion,numeral
alas,incoherent,barrels,arisen,desolation,generosity,furlong,
subserve,restrain,restore,indorsement,disbursement,central,ma-
terial,immaterial,illuminated,eliminated,spiritulist,imperial,
relinquish,reluctant,religion,similar,relation,reliable,chande-
lier,purliew,purloin,earlier.

Idle scholars may be very careless. Careless scholars
seldom win victories in lessons. Lazy scholars make lazy men.
The girl deserves the medal for diligence. We listened cheerfully to the speech of the master. The tailor made a new coat
for the chemist. The story of the uncle was a jest. Summer
has come again. The boy shot the bird in the road. We have
tested the coin several times. The servant may take the lamp
into the parlor. The man took a lump of gold to the chemist.
Last week the snow was deep and the weather was cold. We
might restrain the tempest of destruction. The irresponsible
man was restored to his former position. In the perusal of
the protocol,we observed the allowance made to settlers in the
interior of the land.

NOTE -- As the pupil acquires a knowledge of the principles,he finds his ability to write words constantly enlarging
until he is able,finally,to write everything he hears: but the
reading of what he has written is quite another matter.  Good
reading is acquired only by familiarity·with the outlines of
words,and by facility in phonetic spelling,and analyzing.
    Correct writing is an additional aid to ready reading.
If the pupil makes T's out of all his P's,and S's out of all
his F's neither he nor any one else will ever be able to read
his writing except by guessing from the context.

# CHAPTER XV.

## SYLLABLES BEGINNING AND ENDING WITH THE SAME LETTER.

When a consonant occurs twice in one syllable, as in peep, coke, cloak, etc., the second consonant is often added by beginning or ending the stem with a short, straight tick at a very acute angle to the main stem, thus:

peep, prop, prepare, cake, crock, cook, paper, click, bob.

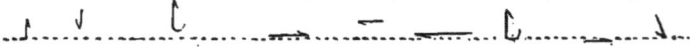

### READING AND WRITING EXERCISE.

Peep, pope, cake, croak, creek, prop, deed, stowed, public, property, preparation, click, altitude, clock, publish, strata, crook, cloak, cog, coke, cook, crack, pepper, improper, proprietor, propriety proportion, proposition, prepossessed, detachment, problem, pebble, paper, pauper, correct, collect, recollect, correctly, keg, propose, proposal, involve, revolve, cricket, frustrate, crocodile, perpetrate, propagate, crockery, peeping, cooking, Baptist, preposterous capable, vivid, stratify, people, papal, recognize, cognition, detaching, detailed, prohibit, prohibition, deduction, treaties, substitute, demented, prepared, church, preponderate, introduction, apoplectic, appropriate, tradition, propensity, probably, propelling, popular, detained, auditor, editor, determine, accumulate, indebted, prostrate, recognition, arbitrate, creditor, immediately, mediate, bobolink.

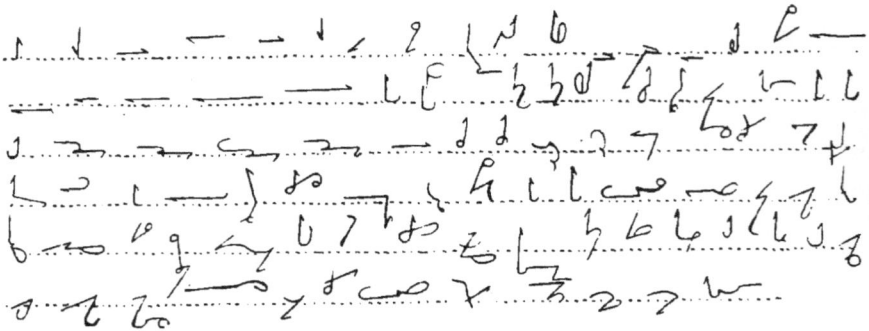

### SENTENCES.

The proprietor lives not far from the creek. For a mo-

ment the old clock on the stairs ceased to tick. Not much ben-
efit was derived from the proposition. For the week I must de
cline the offer. Much opposition was developed from time to
time. The lad shuddered and stared at the beast. The lubber
rowed over to the ship. The graceful player caused a digression in our favor. The charge was not properly published to
the people. The capable editor vividly portrayed the preposterous tradition. We determined to prepare a proper statement
on the ground that it probably might not be recognized as very
frivolous. The pressure upon the piston at the pleasure of
the operator was a great point in its favor. I recollect the
proposal involved a serious charge. We revolved the proposition in our minds. If the forgery is detected, the forger may
spend a term in prison. The immediate cause of the accident
will not probably be determined. The indorser indorsed the
paper, but the indorsement was refused by the cashier.

## THE DOUBLE CONSONANT Q OR ITS EQUIVALENT KW.

The double consonant Q may be represented by a small semi
circle, or by the stems K and W joined, thus:

quit, quake, quite, squarely, quill, queer, quote, quart.

Quay, queen, quire, inquire, acquaint, qualm, quaker, quake,
quick, quickly, quicken, requiem, equal, equality, squire, twirl,
dwarf, dwindle, quarter, squint, squander, quality, bewilder, tran-
quil, exquisite, dwell, beware, bewail, quantity, equanimity, quan-
dary, equipment, tweak, quarreling, quick-silver, persuade, equator,
persuasion, equalize, require, equivalent, equivocate, squarely, re-
quest, squalor, subsequently, quotation, frequently, liquidate,

squeak,squawk.tweed,qualify.qualification.disqualify.

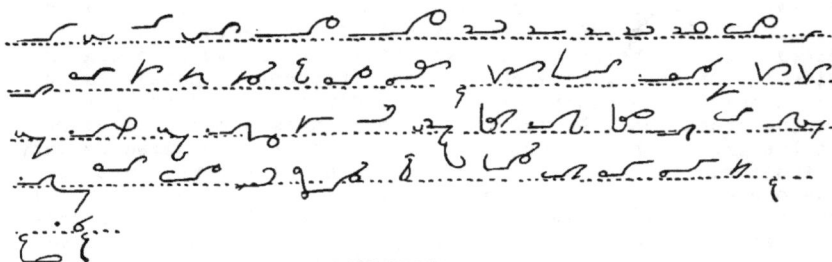

## SENTENCES.

Rome was great only in what we call physical strength.
The waves of sound do not move so rapidly as do the waves of
light. The ancient Roman went to bed early simply his wor-
thy mother earth could not afford him candles. Milk is one
of the most important foods,since it has in it all the ele-
ments of nutrition in the most digestible form. Truth,crush-
ed to earth,will rise again. train up a child in the way he
should go.and,when he is old he will not depart from it.

As the twig is bent,the tree is inclined. As we perceive
the shadow to have moved on the dial,but did not see it move;
and,as it appears that the grass has grown,although nobody
ever saw it grow: so the advances we make in knowledge are
perceivable only by the distance. Our place is to be true to
the best we know. A shrug of the shoulders would lose much
of its significance if it were translated into words.

# SENTENCES.

I am quite at home with the people. We are not inquisitive. The story cannot be true. Quite as much depends upon the quality, as upon the quantity of the wine. She was dressed with exquisite taste. The point of the spear pierced the side of the board. The nobles of Spain are in the states. The door was quickly shut and the rat shot. I owe the men an apology. Iron ore is found in all parts of the world. The isle of Hawiie is an island in the Pacific Ocean. Here are her flowers. The oil-can slipped from the oily grip of the hale and hearty man. Oh! high above the earth are the stars of Heaven. Our share of the wave-washed shore will shortly be shown. She shall hear the charge made public. The queen squandered her revenue. We required from the squire a square and equal denial of the flimsy story. Almost thou persuadest me. I learned subsequently the quarter from whence the quarrel originated. The quality of the equipment was exquisite. Dear Sir, The quotations were favorably received.

# CHAPTER XVI.

## THE STEMS TH AND Y.

The double consonant TH is represented by a shaded curved stem slanted to the right; thus:

the,tha,thah.          thaw,thoe,thoo.

ith,eth,ath.           oth,uth,ooth.

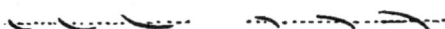

The consonant Y is represented by a small shaded curved stem written in the same direction as the primary vowels. The sound represented by the vowel U,which is the equivalent of Y, is also produced by shading stems at the beginning.

ye,ya,yah.      yaw,yoe,yoo. OR  ye,ya,yah.      yaw,yoe,yoo.

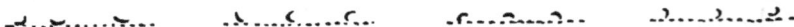

## READING AND WRITING EXERCISE.

The,they,thaw,though,author,other,lath,lather,leather, wrath,rather,thither,hither,heather,heath,hath,there,athletic, Ruth,ye,yea,you,year,yore,your,unite,universal,Europe,young, younger,youth,use,useful,union,humor,human,humanity,unanimous, unique,unanimity,singer,anchor,anger,hunger,hanger,angle,single,link,lank,long,lung,wring,wringer,wrong,ring,rink,rank, rankle,longer,linger,king,cling,spring,drink,think,belong,feeling,ceiling,junction,function,bank,bankrupt,wrangle,thoroughly Thursday,usual,utility,handkerchief,yard,failure,strengthened, atheism,cathedral,arithmetic,yield,yelled,churchyard,authority authorize,hitherto,willingly,reunion,punctuality,uniform,opinion,overthrow,theory,theatre,thunderbolt,enthroned,yonder,yesterday,injunction,value,genuine.

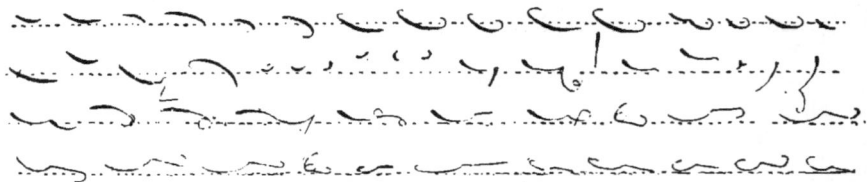

Other people younger than you use the same thing, but not
so strongly; they think it lengthens life. The angry storm
blows the singers hither and thither. Refreshing showers have
long been falling. The thirsty earth greedily drinks them up
For years the angry man hungered for human sympathy. Not a
single Thursday did he miss till yesterday. Yonder lean,long,
lank,and hungry looking knave lingered near the pump in the
yard. We are uniformly of the opinion this unfeeling wrangle
will no longer yield to proper authority. We are feeling rather angry at the author of the song sung at the theatre. It
was not singing; it was yelling. I shall willingly yield to
the higher authority. My rank is not so high as yours. They
still linger in Europe. The youth as usual shall learn to
ring the bell alone. We were very fortunate,while the others
were very unfortunate. In union there is strength. United
we stand,divided we fall. Beyond yon mountain lies a fertile
valley. The assembly agreed unanimously.

# THE PREFIX CON AND COM.

The prefix CON is represented by a light dot at the beginning or the end of a stem; CONT or COND are represented by a light tick or dash instead of the dot.

The prefix COM and COMP or COMB are represented by a shaded dot and dash respectively.

DECON,DISCON,INCON,etc,are represented by disjoining the stems,and writing the second stem directly under the middle of the first.

## READING AND WRITING EXERCISE.

Contain,comfort,connection,composition,conceit,contention,compass,commit,conditional,discomfort,disconcert,decomposed,decomposition,country,county,conceal,council,conception,consider,contempt,confession,concern,commendation,complimentary,constant,conceivable,complaint,compressible,constraint,consummation,conscientious,conquest,contradict,congress,conduct,contract,contact,contaminate,controversy,controvert,context,continue,contingent,condemn,condescend,inconstant,incomparable,incomprehensible,unconditional,incommode,incomplete,incompetent,inconceivable,incongrous,inconsistant,uncontrollable,unconcerned,compensation,communication,incontestible,inconvenient,contents,construction,consequently,convinced,compound,comfortable,consumer,comet,commissioner,commercial,compilation,conform,confirmation,contrary,commentary,congregation,conclusion,contribute,contribution,consciousness,comic,discontinue,continental,complete,dompetition,conversation,commonwealth,conversion,commensurate,congratulate,conscience,conscious,unconsciously,continuance,reconsider.

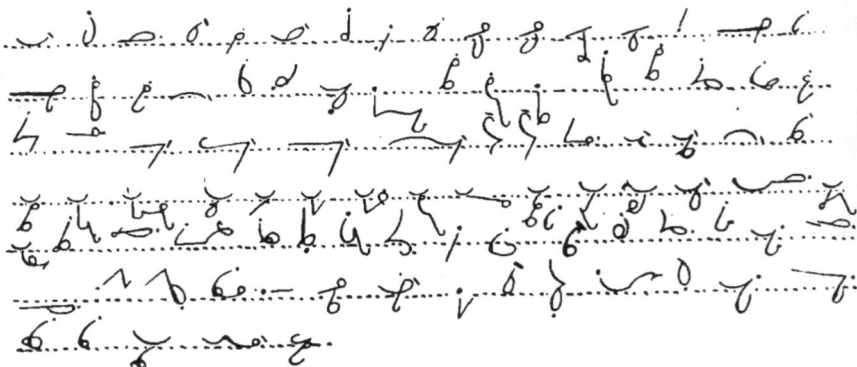

Period. colon. interrogation, semicolon. comma.

## SENTENCES.

The slothful man shook off his lethargy, and slaked his thirst at the true fountain of knowledge. We are pleased to acknowledge your very favorable reply. Gentlemen:- You are requested to favor us with a letter containing a brief list of quotations at your earliest convenience. Please communicate to us the commercial footing of George Smith & Co. All communications shall be strictly confidential. It is quite necessary for all telegrams of importance to be quickly confirmed by letter. Concerning the compensation required, we are at present unable to state positively. They demand shorter hours of labor.

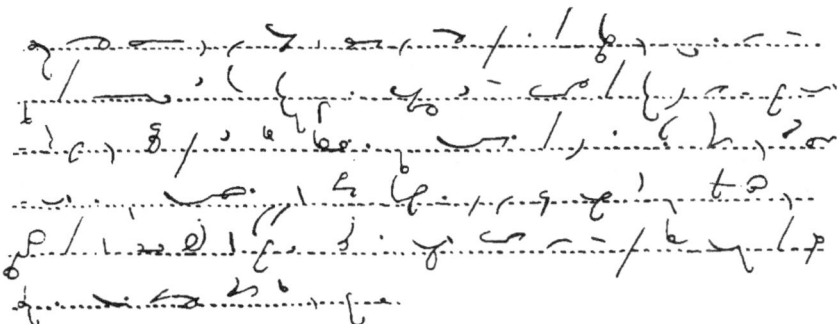

CAUTION.-- Many pupils find great difficulty in writing the stems P and F correctly, the tendency being to slant them like the T and the S stem. If the pupil finds himself falling into that error, he should break himself of the habit at once by devoting special attention to writing those stems correctly.

# CHAPTER XVII

## EXPEDIENTS.

The principles developed up to this point are sufficient to enable a person of ordinary intelligence to reach a very high rate of speed by proper practice. To facilitate a still higher rate of speed, various expedients are employed as follows:
When the stem barely cuts the line, it ends with T or D; thus;

bit,bet,bat.　bot,but,boot.

vete,vate,vat.　vot,vote,voot.　vite,voit,vout.

ipt,ept,apt.　opt,upt,oopt.

ift,eft,aft.　oft,uft,ooft.

sit,set,sat.　sot,sut,soot.

lift,left,laft.　loft,luft,looft.

idged,edged,adged.　odged,udged,oodged.

kid,ked,kad.　kod,kud,kood.

mete,mate,mat.　mot,mote,moot.　mite,moit,mout.

licked,lecked,lacked.　locked,lucked,loocked.

rikt,rckt,rakt.    rokt,rukt,rookt.

EXERCISE.

Beautiful,introduce,receipt,outstandings,middlings,enter-
prise,intermediate,rebate,indignity,speedily,Eastern,outward,
notify,pattern,industrious,anticipated,international,medium,
esteemed,estimate,estimation,butter,better,butterfly,neatly,
natural,matter,intention,afternoon,aptly,obtain,intimated,
modify,modification,undertaken,notwithstanding,affidavit,en-
deavor,actually,undertake,imbedded,indifferent,interrupted,in-
dispensable,evidently,entitled,entertainingly,remittance,limit
limited,middle,meddle,midst,undoubtedly,intelligence,tightly,
doubtless.

Your esteemed favor at hand.  We handle only first-class
articles.  All night the dreadless Angel,unpursued,through
Heaven's wide champaign held his way,till Morn,waked by the
circling hours,with rosy hand unbarred the gates of light.
The unfortunate inmates were treated with commendable humanity.

T OR D OMITTED.

In words of two or more syllables,T or D is often omitted
where such omission does not impair the legibility of the word

Gratify,gratitude,grateful,predicate,prodigal,certainly,
uncertain,respectfully,inevitable,absolutely,rectify,multiply,
multitude,predict,protect,article.

# THE PREFIX X.

The prefix may be indicated by a small loop at the beginning of a stem; thus:

Exalt,exult,exact,exaggerate,exactly,examine,example,exasperate,excavate,exceed,excel,excellent,eccentric,except,accept,exchange,excise,excite,exclaim,exclamation,excuse,execute excessive,accident,excommunicate,excruciate,exculpate,executrix,executor,exempt,exert,exercise,exertion,exile,exist,exhort,exonerate,exorbitant,expand,expend,expatiate,expense,expect,expedient,expire,expiration,expert,exportation,expeditious,explain,explore,express,explode,expose,expulsion,exquisite,extant,extend,extemporary,extract,extraordinary,exhibition,exhibit,extremity,excellence,extinguished,extinct,exhausted,extirpate,expound,executive,exploit,exterior.

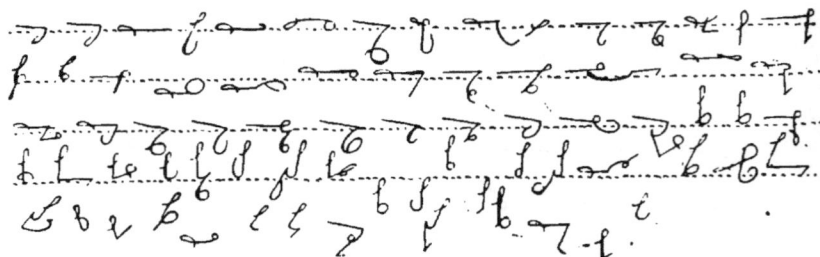

## MISCELLANEOUS EXERCISE.

Some of the following frequently recurring words are not written exactly in accordance with the principles,but are abbreviated in various ways for speed:

Carefully,carry,established,especial,permit,party,particular,economy,large,enlarge,discharge,liberty,satisfaction,satisfy,unreasonable,economical,stability,stipulate,accumulation,accompany,accommodate,familiar,submit,realize,alcohol,accordingly,spiritous,first,distinctly,distinguish,value,valuation,annual,suggestion,supply,apply,perhaps,volume,admit,confirm,satisfactory,somewhat,nevertheless,further,turn,forth,according,permission,carpenter,transmit,transmission,northerly,interested,southerly,easterly,westerly,overwhelm,literally,literary,alacrity,accurate,absolutely,accuracy,valuable,whomsoever,transport,transact,responsible,transgress,transcend,transfigure,righteousness,particularly,curiously.

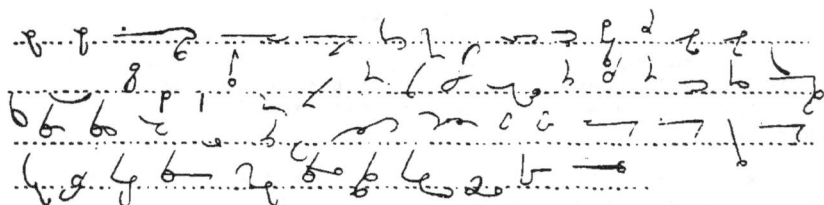

**MEMORIAL DAY.** -- A holiday always points back to an important history. It is not necessary or judicious to prate too long or too often even of very important events of the past; but Memorial Day, as long as it lasts, must always be an anniversary to bring many a weary sigh, and start many a bitter memory.

It was the youth, the beautiful, hopeful, courageous youth, that in all the glory of their fresh young lives went forth in large numbers in those mournful days to do battle for their own dear land. Let us ever bear in mind that it is to many of them who yielded up their precious lives in the cause of unity, freedom, and justice that the youth of to-day are already indebted for their freedom, and the peace and the strong bands of union that characterize us as a people.

Cover the graves of the soldiers with flowers, that we may keep green the memory of our heroic dead, and that we may again learn the holy lesson of patriotism.--Selected.

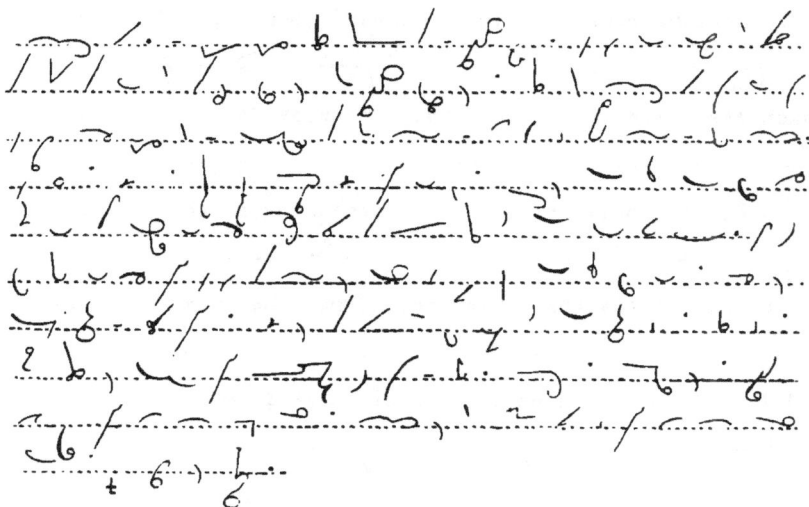

# CHAPTER XVIII

The words OF and TO,and the phrases OF THE,OF A,TO THE
and TO A are frequently omitted in rapid writing,and the omission indicated by writing the preceding and following word
close together.

In phrase-writing,the sign A or AN,and AND are used in-
terchangeably when joined to other words,the context prevent-
ing any confusion.

## PHRASES AND ABBREVIATIONS.

In the,in a,on the,on a, and the,and a,that,made,with,on,

meke,came or come,might,could,good,not,anything,nothing,with-

out,shall,should,between,next,much,which,isn't,thing,think,

I was,he is,he was,it is,it was,I'd,I don't,was not,also,I

would have,he would have,wasn't,hasn't,musn't,at first,at once,

which was,which it was,to hand,at hand,as far as,we would be

pleased,what would,we would have,something,forgotten,that it

has been,that the,that this,from a,from the,from it,our own,

and I could not,with which,without which,it may be,it cannot be,for it was,had been,in all the,and he was,but he was,and

was,are in,or in,a good deal,a great deal,a good many,a great

many,and yet,yet it was,has been,it has been,as possible,after

that,so that the,as it was,with which it was,less then,more

than,it would be,but,been,this,more or less,I have seen,we

have seen,and I cannot,and we can,I think not,I will not have,

we will not,shall not,shall be,will not have,for this is,this

is,in receipt,in reply,in reference,in regard,shall see,shall

it,it is not,what has been,they have been,there have been,

there are,there will be,there must be,it must be,I may be, I

may have been,you have,you will be,you can,you may be,you are,

your own,with much,without much,are not,did not,did you have,

did you ever,how long have,was it,is it,does it,it seems,do

you remember,you see,we are in receipt,your favor,I am in receipt,we remain,we beg to say,we beg to acknowledge,I beg to

say.

-------

    NOTE-- No rules can be formulated for phrasing. Words
may be joined in infinitum.care being taken to join only such
words as run easily together. The best writers,however,seldom
join more than two or three words in one phrase.


LETTER.

    Dear Sirs:---We received from you on the 22nd inst.,by
Adam,s Express,a tin can tightly soldered,and marked by a label posted on top,"T.H.N.& Co,Warranted Strictly Pure White-
Lead." In order to ascertain the true mineral composition of
the paint contained in the can,we dissolved away the oil with
which the paint had been ground,by neutral solvents,and sub-
jected the remaining dry paint to chemical analysis.
    The dry paint contained 97 1-2 per cent.of dry white-lead
of the usual composition,the remainder of 2 1-2 per cent.
being moisture,a slight residue of oil,and traces of foreign
matter,as is the case with all pure white-lead. We tested
for imputities,and found none. The paint in the above can
is what its label alleges it to be,namely,"Strictly Pure White
Lead." We return you the paint by Adam's Express,reserving a
sample of it for ourselves.
                    Respectfully yours,

Adrian, Mich. December 1,1895

Albert   J. Post.Esq.

Box 620,Carnagie,Pa.

Dear Sir:

        Replying to your letter of November 24th,permit

us to enclose you prices and styles of our fencing.  We

hope you will take pains to look this printed matter over

carefully,and ask of us any further information you may de-

sire.  We have no dealer in your vicinity,and we shall be

glad to give you a reasonable discount,should you conclude

to buy. Awaiting your further correspondence hopefully,we

remain,

        Yours very truly

NOTE.-- From this point in the pupil's course,he should
commence a thorough and systematic-review of the principles,in
connection with his general practice of the shorthand exercises contained in the following pages. One page should be
taken at a time,and practiced till it can be written at a
rate of 100 to 150 words per minute.  This copious practice,
together with a thorough knowledge of the principles,is sufficient to make a good general writer.

Those who desire a more extended course.of practice for
the purpose of reaching a high rate of speed,or of following a
any particular line of reporting,should procure Part Second,
and write each page of shorthand contained therein,from dictation,no  less than thirty times.   They should also study
carefully the models of proper forms for commercial and legal
documents,such as Deeds,Articles of Agreement,Specifications,
Bids on Contracts,etc.

Pupils preparing themselves for business letter-writing
should devote their attention chiefly to the business letters,the large number of which contained in Part Second were
Collected from the best business houses of the United States
and England.

## THE OLD CURIOSITY SHOP.

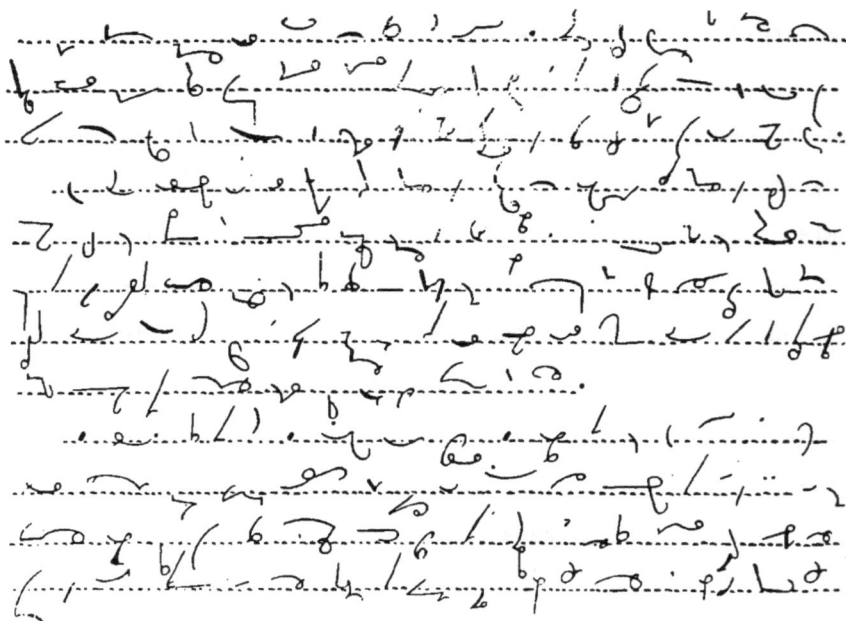

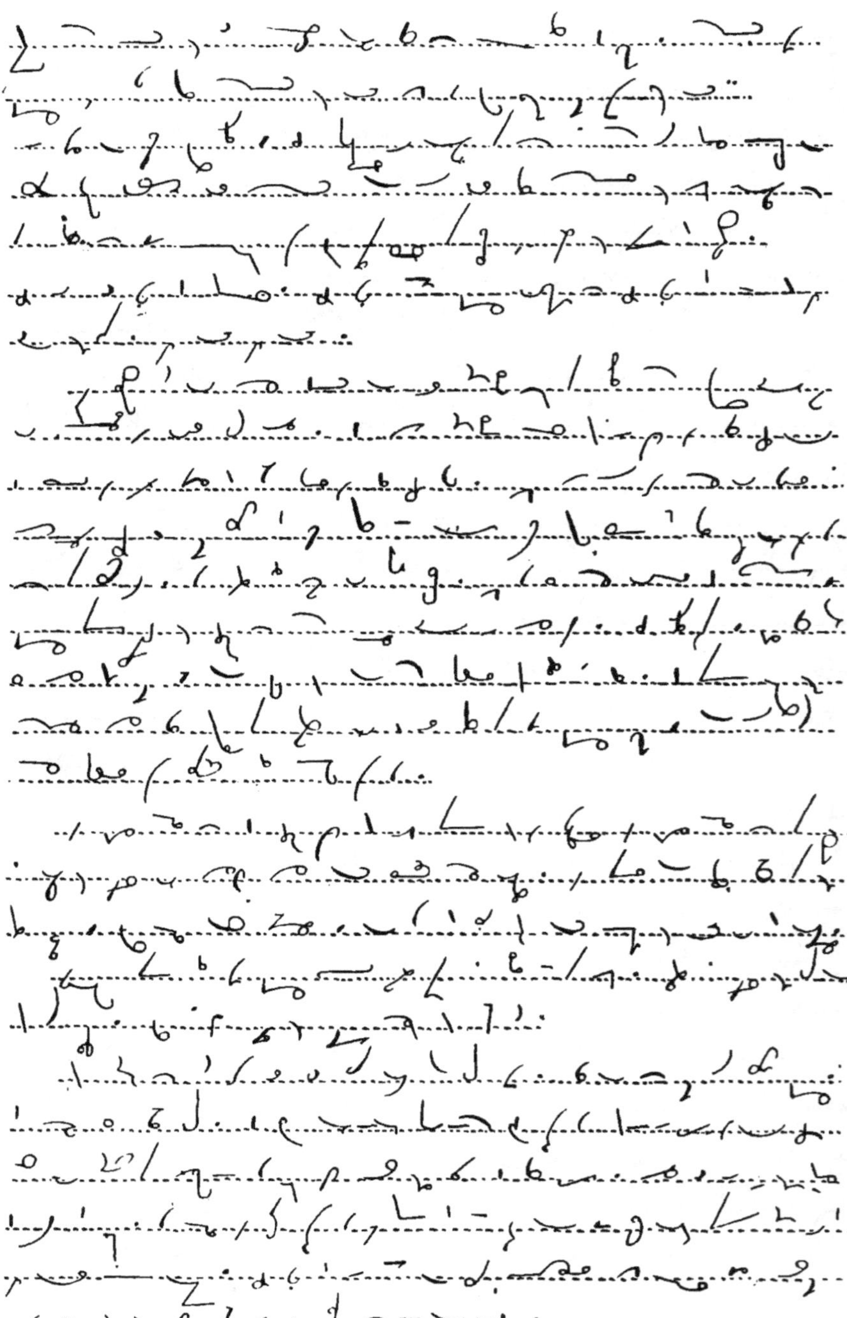

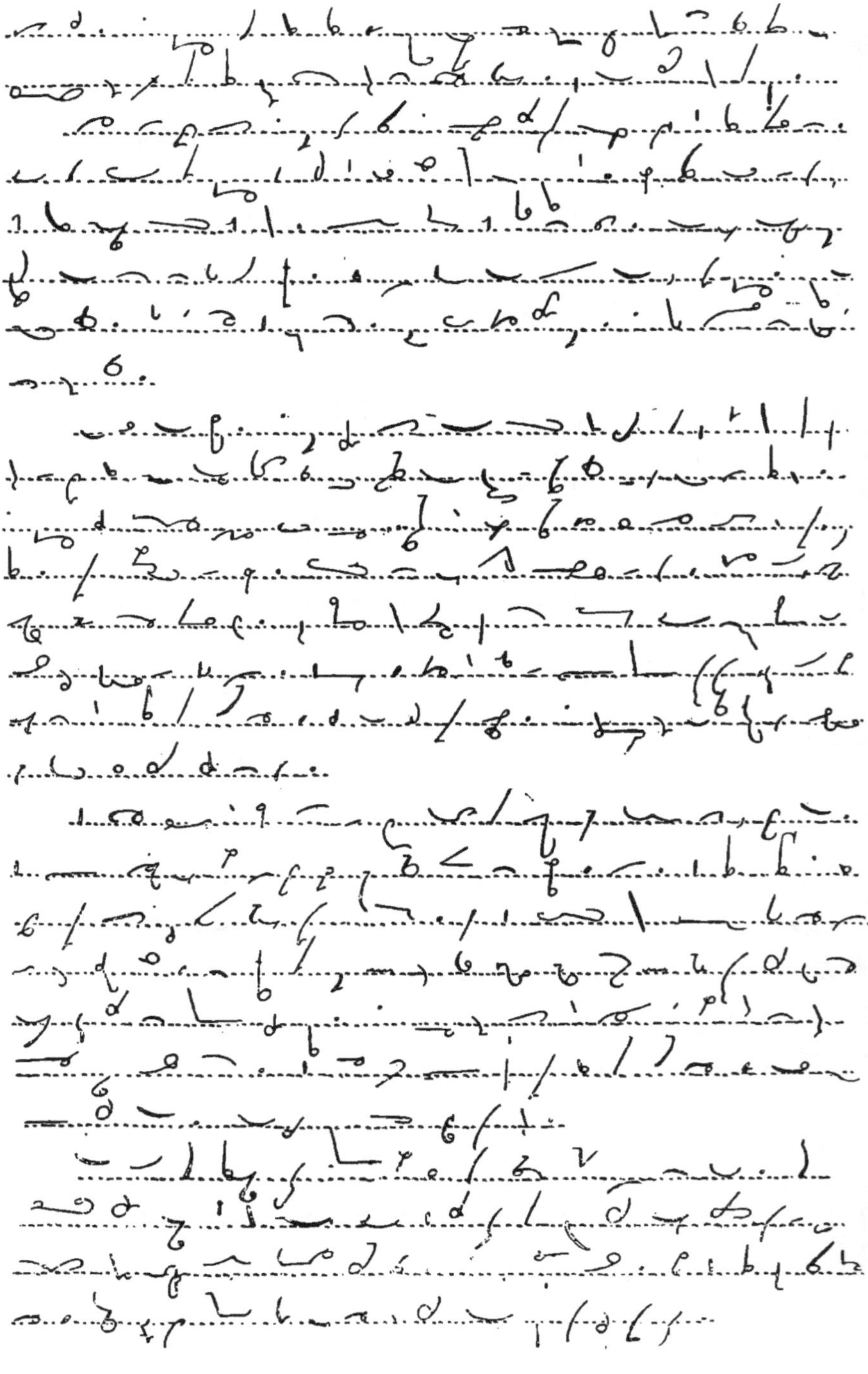

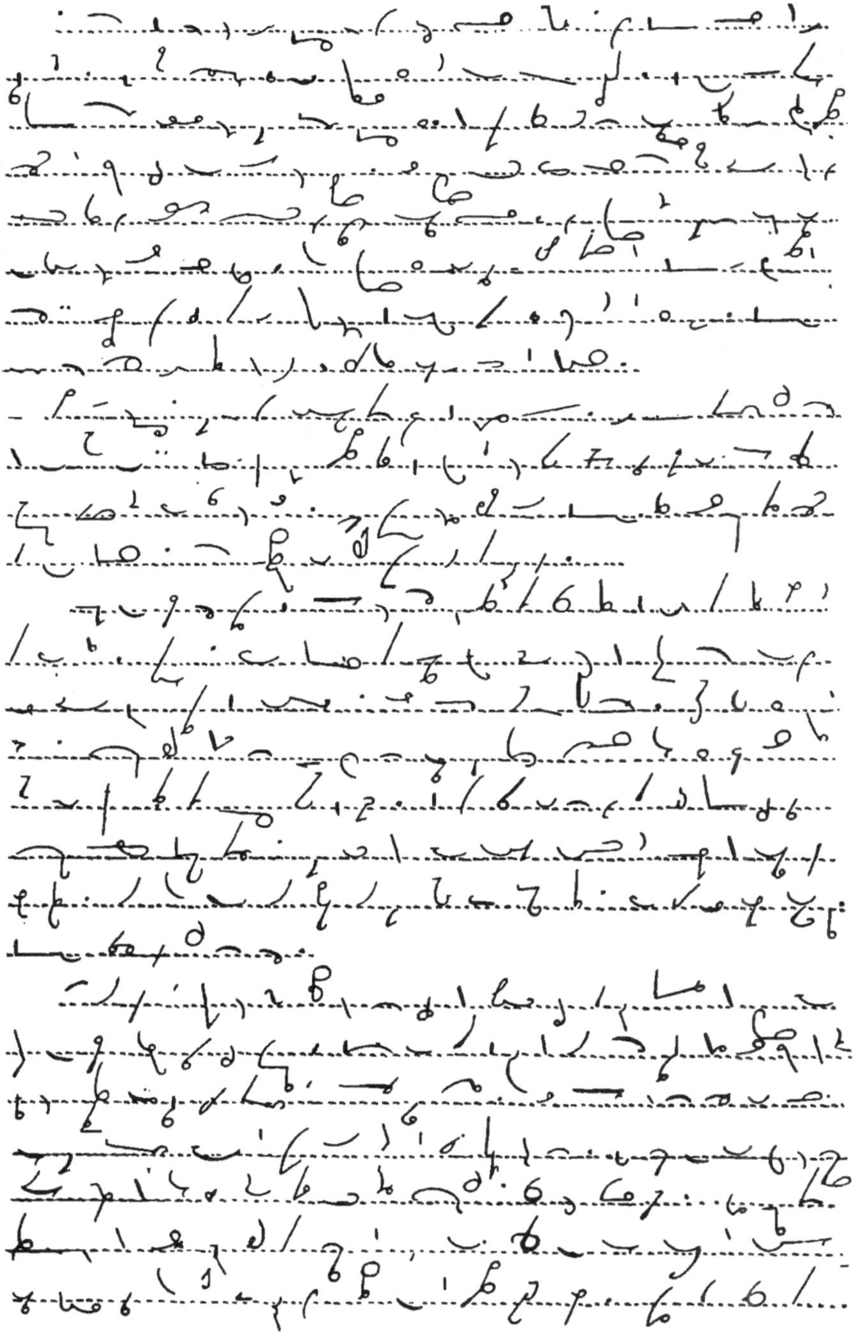

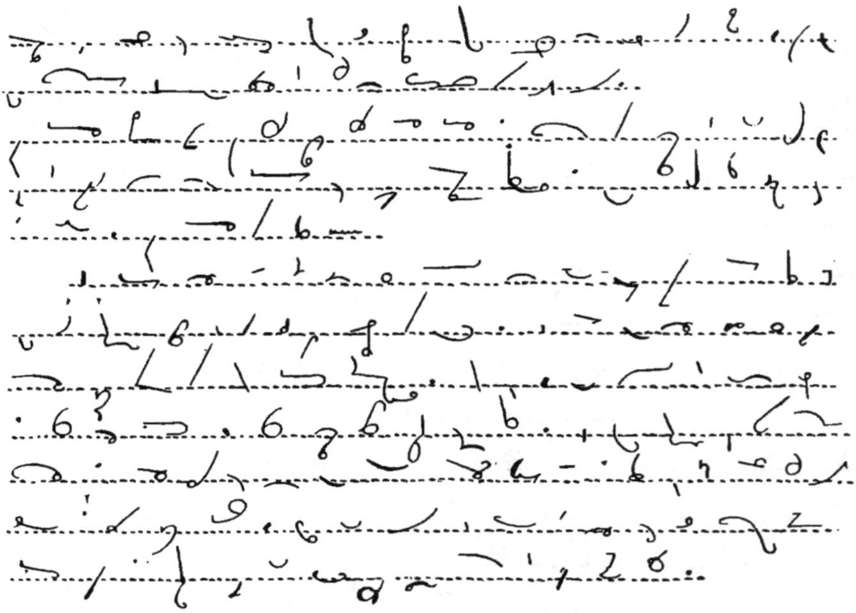

# THE OLD CURIOSITY SHOP.

Although I am an old man night is generally my time for
walking. In the summer I often leave home early in the morning and roam about the fields and lanes all day,or even escape
for days or weeks together; but,saving in the country,I seldom
go out until after dark,though,Heaven be thanked,I love its
light,and feel the cheerfulness it sheds upon the earth,as
much as any creature living.

I have fallen insensibly into this habit,both because it
favors my infirmity,and because it affords me greater opportunity of speculating upon the characters and occupations of
those who fill the streets. The glare and hurry of broad noon
are not adapted to idle pursuits like mine; a glimpse of passing faces caught by the light of a street lamp,or a shop window,is often better for my purpose than their full revelation
in the daylight; and,if I must add the truth,night is kinder
in this respect than day,which too often destroys an air-built
castle at the moment of its completion,without the least ceremony or remorse.

That constant pacing to and fro,that never-ending rest-
lessness,that incessant tread of feet wearing the rough stones
smooth and glossy—is it not a wonder how the dwellers in nar-
row ways can bear to hear it? Think of a sick man,in such a
place as Saint Martin's Court,listening to the footsteps,and,
in the midst of pain and weariness,obliged,despite himself (as
though it were a task he must perform),to detect the child's
step from the man's,the slipshod beggar from the booted exquisite,the lounging from the busy,the dull heel of the saun-
tering outcast from the quick tread of an expectant pleasure-
seeker think of the hum and noise being always present to his
senses,and of the stream of life that will not stop,pouring
on,on,on,through all his restless dreams,as if he were con-
demned to lie,dead but conscious,in a noisy church-yard,and
had no hope of rest for centuries to come.

Then,the crowds forever passing and repassing on the
bridges (on those which are free of toll at least),where many
stop on fine evenings looking listlessly down upon the water,
with some vague idea that by and by it runs between green
banks which grow wider and wider until at last it joins the
broad vast sea—where some halt to rest from heavy loads,and
think,as they look over the parapet,that to smoke and lounge
away one's life,and lie sleeping in the sun upon a hot tar-
paulin,in a dull,slow,sluggish barge must be happiness unalloy
ed—and where some,and a very different class,pause with heavier
loads than they,remembering to have heard or read in some old
time that drowning was not a hard death,but of all means of

7

suicide the easiest and best.

Covent Garden Market at sunrise,too,in the spring or
summer,when the fragrance of sweet flowers is in the air,over-
powering even the unwholesome streams of last night's debauch-
ery,and driving the dusky thrush,whose cage has hung outside a
garret window all night long,half mad with joy.  Poor bird!
the only neighboring thing at all akin to the other little cap-
tives,some of whom,shrinking from the hot hands of drunken pur-
chasers,lie drooping on the path already,while others,soddened
by close contact,await the time when they shall be watered and
freshened up to please more sober company,and make old clerks
who pass them on their road to business wonder what has filled
their breasts with visions of the country.

But my present purpose is not to expatiate upon my walks.
The story I am about to relate arose out of one of these ram-
bles,and thus I have been led to speak of them by way of pre-
face.

One night I had roamed into the city and was walking slow
ly on in my usual way,musing upon a great many things,when I
was arrested by an inquiry,the purport of which did not reach
me,but seemed to be addressed to myself,and was preferred in a
soft,sweet voice that struck me very pleasantly.  I turned
hastily around,and found at my elbow a pretty little girl who
begged to be directed to a certain street at a considerable
distance,and,indeed,in quite another quarter of the town.

"It is a very long way from here," said I, "my child."

"I know that,sir;" she replied,timidly.  "I am afraid it
is a very long way,for I came from there to-night."

"Alone?" said I,in some surprise.

"Oh,yes, I don't mind that; but I am a little frightened
now,for I have lost my road."

"And what made you ask it of me?  Suppose I should tell
you wrong?"

"I am sure you will not do that," said the little creature
"you are such a very old gentlemen,and walk so slow yourself."

I cannot describe how much I was impressed by this appeal
and the energy with which it was made,which brought a tear into the child's clear eye,and made her slight figure tremble as
she looked up into my face.

"Come," said I, "I'll take you there."

She put her hand in mine as confidingly as if she had
known me from her cradle,and we trudged away together,the
little creature accommodating her pace to mine, and rather
seeming to lead and take care of me than I to be protecting her.
I observed that every now and then she stole a curious look at
my face as if to make sure that I was not deceiving her,and
that these glances (very sharp and keen they were too) seemed
to increase her confidence at every repetition.

For my part,my curiosity and interest were at least equal
to the child's,for child she certainly was,although I thought

it probable from what I could make out that her very small and delicate frame imparted a peculiar youthfulness to her appearance. Though more scantily attired than she might have been she was dressed with perfect neatness and betrayed no marks of poverty or neglect.

"Who has sent you so far by yourself?" said I.

"Somebody who is very kind to me,sir."

"And what have you been doing?"

"That I must not tell," said the child.

There was something in the manner of this reply which caused me to look at the little creature with an involuntary expression of surprise,for I wondered what kind of errand it might be that occasioned her to be prepared for questioning. Her quick eye seemed to read my thoughts. As it met mine she added that there was no harm in what she had been doing,but it was a great secret which she did not even know herself.

This was said with no appearance of cunning or deceit,but with an unsuspicious frankness that bore the impress of truth. She walked on as before,growing more familiar with me as we proceeded,and talking cheerfully by the way,but she said no more about her home,beyond remarking that we were going quite a new road,and asking if it were a short one.

While we were thus engaged I revolved in my mind a hundred explanations of the riddle,and rejected them every one. I really felt ashamed to take advantage of the ingenuousness or grateful feeling of the child for the purpose of gratifying my curiosity. I love these little people,and it is not a slight thing when they,who are so fresh from God,love us. As I had felt pleased,at first,by her confidence,I determined to deserve it,and to do credit to the nature which had prompted her to repose it in me.

There was no reason,however,why I should refrain from seeing the person who had inconsiderately sent her to so great a distance by night and alone; and,as it was not improbable that if she found herself near home she might take farewell of me and deprive me of the opportunity,I avoided the most frequented ways and took the most intricate. Thus it was not until we arrived in the street itself that she knew where we were. Clapping her hands with pleasure,and running on before me for a short distance,my little acquaintance stopped at a door,and remaining on the step till I came up,knocked at it when I joined her.

A part of the door was of glass.unprotected by any shutter; which I did not observe at first,for all was very dark and silent within,and I was anxious ( as indeed the child was also ) for an answer to her summons. When she had knocked twice or thrice,there was a noise as if some person were moving inside,and at length a faint light appeared through the glass which,as it approached very slowly  the bearer having to make his way through a great many scattered articles  enabled

me to see,both what kind of a person it was who advanced,and
what kind of a place it was through which he came.

He was a little old man,with long gray hair,whose face
and figure,as he held the light above his head and looked before him as he approached,I could plainly see. Though much
altered by age,I fancied I could recognize in his spare and
slender form something of that delicate mold which I noticed
in the child. Their bright blue eyes were certainly alike,but
his face was so deeply furrowed,and so very full of care,that
here all resemblance ceased.

The place through which he made his way at leisure was
one of those receptacles for old and curious things which seem
to crouch in odd corners of this town,and to hide their musty
treasures from the public eye in jealousy and distrust. There
were suits of mail standing like ghosts in armor,here and
there; fantastic carvings brought from monkish cloisters; rus-
ty weapons of various kinds; distorted figures in china,and
wood,and iron,and ivory; tapestry,and strange furniture that
might have been designed in dreams. The haggard aspects of
the little old man was wonderfully suited to the place; he
might have groped among old churches,and tombs,and deserted
houses,and gathered all the spoils with his own hands. There
was nothing in the whole collection but was in keeping with
himself; nothing that looked older or more worn than he.

As he turned the key in the lock,he surveyed me with
some astonishment,which was not diminished when he looked from
me to my companion. The door being opened,the child addressed
him as her grandfather,and told him the little story of our
companionship.

"Why bless thee,child," said the old man,patting her on
the head, "how couldst thou miss thy way? What if I had lost
thee,Nell!"

"I would have found my way back to you,grandfather," said
the child,boldly: "never fear."

The old man kissed her; then turned to me and begged me
to walk in. I did so. The door was closed and locked. Preceding me with a light,he led me through the place I had already seen from without,into a small sitting-room behind,in
which was another door opening into a kind of closet,where I
saw a little bed that a fairy might have slept in,it looked so
very small and was so prettily arranged. The child took a
candle and tripped into this little room,leaving the old man
and me together.

"You must be tired,sir," said he,as he placed a chair near
the fire; how can I thank you?"

"By taking more care of your grandchild another time,my
good friend," I replied.

"More care!" said the old man in a shrill voice,"more care
of Nelly! why who ever loved a child as I love Nell?"

He said this with such evident surprise,that I was per-

plexed what answer to make; the more so,because coupled with
something feeble and wandering in his manner,there were,in his
face,marks of deep and anxious thought which convinced me that
he could not be,as I had been at first inclined to suppose,in
a state of dotage or imbecility.

"I don't think you consider   " I began.

"I don't consider!" cried the old man,interrupting me," I
don't consider her! ah,how little you know of the truth! Little Nelly,little Nelly!"

It would be impossible for any man  I care not what his
form of speech might be  to express more affection than the
dealer in curiosities did in these four words.  I waited for
him to speak again,but he rested his chin upon his hand,and,
shaking his head twice or thrice,fixed his eyes upon the fire.

While we were sitting thus,in silence,the door of the closet opened,and the child returned; her light brown hair hang-
ing loose about her neck,and her face flushed with the haste
she had made to rejoin us.  She busied herself immediately in
preparing supper.  While she was thus engaged I remarked that
the old man took an opportunity of observing me more closely
than he had done yet.  I was surprised to see,that,all this
time,every thing was done by the child,and that there appeared
to be no other persons but ourselves in the house.  I took advantage of a moment when she was absent to venture a hint on
this point,to which the old man replied that there were few
grown persons as trustworthy or as careful as she.

"It always grieves me," I observed,roused by what I took
to be his selfishness: "it always grieves me to contemplate
the initiation of children into the ways of life,when they are
scarcely more than infants.  It checks their confidence and
simplicity  two of the best qualities that Heaven gives them
and demands that they share our sorrows before they are capable of entering into our enjoyments.

"It will never check hers," said the old man,looking
steadily at me,"the springs are too deep.  Besides the children of the poor know but few pleasures.  Even the cheap de-
lights of childhood must be bought and paid for."

"But  forgive me for saying this  you are surely not so
very poor  " said I.

"She is not my child,sir," returned the old man.  "Her
mother was,and she was poor.  I save nothing  not a penny
though I love as you see,but"  he laid his hand upon my arm
and leaned forward to wisper  "she shall be rich one of these
days,and a fine lady.  Don't you think ill of me because I use
her help.  She gives it cheerfully,as you see,and it would
break her heart if she knew that I suffered any body else to
do for me what her little hands could undertake  I don't consider!" he cried,with sudden querulousness,"why,God knows
that this one child is the thought and object of my life,and
yet he never prospers me  no,never!"

At this juncture the subject of our conversation again

returned,and the old man,motioning me to approach the table,
broke off,and said no more.
We had scarcely begun our repast when there was a knock at
the door by which I had entered,and Nell,bursting into a hearty laugh,which I was rejoiced to hear,for it was child-like
and full of hilarity,said it was no doubt dear old Kit come
back at last.
      "Foolish Nell!" said the old man,fondling with her hair.
"She always laughs at poor Kit."
      The child laughed again,more heartily than before,and I
could not help smiling from pure sympathy.  The little old
man took up a candle and went to open the door.  When he came
back,Kit was at his heels.
      Kit was a shock-headed,shambling,awkward lad,with an un-
commonly wide mouth,very red cheeks,a turned-up nose,and certainly the most comical expression of face I ever saw.  He
stopped short at the door on seeing a stranger,twirled in his
hand a perfectly round old hat without any vestige of a brim,
and,resting himself now on one leg,and now on the other, and
changing them constantly,stood in the door-way,looking into
the parlor with the most extraordinary leer I ever beheld.  I
entertained a grateful feeling toward the boy from that minute
for I felt that he was the comedy of the child's life.
      "A long way,wasn't it,Kit?" said the little old man.
      "Why,then,it was a goodish stretch,master," returned Kit.
      "Did you find the house easily?"
      "Why,then,not over and above easy,master," said Kit.
      "Of course you have come back hungry?"
      "Why,then,I do consider myself rather so,master," was the
answer.
      The lad had a remarkable manner of standing sideways as
he spoke,and thrusting his head forward over his shoulder,as
if he could not get at his voice without that accompanying ac-
tion.  I think he would have amused one anywhere,but the
child's exquisite enjoyment of his oddity,and the relief it
was to find that there was something she associated with meriment,in a place that appeared so unsuited to her,were quite
irresistible.  It was a great point,too,that Kit himself was
flattered by the sensation he created,and after several efforts to preserve his gravity,burst into a loud roar,and so
stood with his mouth wide open and his eyes nearly shut,laugh-
ing violently.
      The old man had again relapsed into his former abstrac-
tion,and took no notice of what passed; but I remarked that
when her laugh was over,the child's bright eyes were dimmed
with tears,called forth by the fullness of heart with which
she welcomed her uncouth favorite after the little anxiety of
the night.  As for Kit himself (whose laugh had been one all
the time of that sort which very little would change into a
cry),he carried a large slice of bread and meat and a mug of
beer into a corner,and applied himself to disposing of them

with great voracity.

"Ah!" said the old man,turning to me with a sigh,as if I had spoken to him but that moment,"you don't consider her."

"You must not attach too great weight to a remark founded on first appearances,my friend,"·said I.

"No," returned the old man,thoughtfully, "no. Come hither Nell."

The little girl hastened from her seat and put her arm about his neck.

"Do I love thee,Nell?" said he. ̣ "Say; do I love thee,Nell or no?"

The child only answered by her caresses,and laid her head upon his breast.

"Why dost thou sob?" said the grandfather,pressing her closer to him and glancing toward me. "Is it because thou knowest I love thee,and dost not like that I should seem to doubt it by my question? Well,well then let us say I love dearly.'

"Indeed,indeed you do," replied the child,with great earnestness; "Kit knows you do."

Kit,who,in dispatching his bread and meat,had been swallowing two-thirds of his knife at every mouthful with the coolness of a juggler,stopped short in his operations on being thus appealed to,and bawled,"Nobody isn't such a fool as to say he doesn't," after which he incapacitated himself for furtherconversation by taking a most prodigious sandwich at one bite.

"She is poor now," said the old man,patting the child's cheek,"but,I say again,the time is coming when she shall be rich. It has been a long time coming,but it must come at last a very long time,but it surely must come. It has come to other men who do nothing but waste and riot. When will it come to me?"

"I am very happy as I am,grandfather," said the child.

"Tush,tush!" returned the old man,"thou dost not know how shouldst thou!" Then he muttered again between his teeth,"The time must come,I am very sure it must. It will be all the better for coming late;" and then he sighed and fell into his former musing state,and still holding the child between his knees appeared to be insensible to everything around him. By this time it wanted but a few minutes of midnight,and I arose to go,which recalled him to himself.

"One moment,sir," he said. "Now,Kit near midnight,boy, and you still here! Get home,get home,and be true to your time in the morning,for there's work to do.· Good night! There bid him good night,Nell,and let him be gone!'"

"Good night,Kit," said the child,her eyes lighting up with meriment and kindness.

"Good night,Miss Nell," returned the boy.

"And thank this gentlemen," interposed the old man,"but for whose care I might have lost my little girl to-night."

"No,no,master," said Kit, "that won't do,that won't."

"What do you mean?" cried the old man.

"I'd have found her,master," said Kit; "I'd have found her
I'd bet that I'd find her if she was above ground.  I would,
as quick as any body,master."

Once more opening his mouth and shutting his eyes,and
laughing like a stentor,Kit gradually backed to the door,and
roared himself out.

Free from the room,the boy was not slow in taking his departure; when he had gone,and the child was occupied in clear-
ing the table,the old man said:

"I haven't seemed to thank you,sir,enough for what you
have done to-night,but I do thank you humbly and heartily; and
so does she, and her thanks are better worth than mine.  I
should be sorry that you went away and thought I was unmindful
of your goodness,or careless of her  I am not,indeed."

I was sure of that,I said,from what I had seen.

"But," I added,"may I ask you a question?"

"Ay,sir," replied the old man; "what is it?"

"This delicate child," said I,"with so much beauty and intelligence  has she nobody to care for her but you?  Has she
no other companion or adviser?"

"No," he returned,looking anxiously in my face,"no,and
she wants no other."

"But are you not fearful," said I, "that you may misunder-
stand a charge so tender?  I am sure you mean well,but are you
quite certain that you know how to execute such a trust as
this?  I am an old man like you,and I am actuated by an old
man's concern in all that is young and promising.  Do you not
think that what I have seen of you and this little creature
to-night must have an interest not wholly free from pain?"

"Sir," replied the old man,after a moment's silence,"I
have no right to feel hurt at what you say.  It is true that
in many respects I am the child,and she the grown person  that
you have seen already.  But waking or sleeping,by night or day
in sickness or health,she is the one object of my care: and
if you knew of how much care,you would look on me with differ
ent eyes,you would,indeed.  Ah! it's a weary life for an old
man  a weary,weary life  but there is a great end to gain,and
that I keep before me."

Seeing that he was in a state of excitement and impa-
tience,I returned to put on an outer coat which I had thrown
off on entering the room,purposing to say no more.  I was surprised to see the child standing patiently by,with a cloak upon her arm,and in her hand a hat and stick.

"Those are not mine,my dear," said I.

"No," returned the child quietly," they are grandfather's"

"But he is not going out to-night."

"O yes he is," said the child with a smile.

"And what becomes of you,my pretty one!"

"Me! I stay here of course.  I always do."

I looked in astonishment toward the old man, but he was, or feigned to be, busied in the arrangement of his dress. From him, I looked back to the slight gentle figure of the child. Alone! In that gloomy old place all the long dreary night!

She evinced no consciousness of my surprise, but cheerfully helped the old man with his cloak, and when he was ready took a candle to light us out. Finding that we did not follow as she expected, she looked back with a smile and waited for us. The old man showed by his face that he plainly understood the cause of my hesitation, but he merely signed to me with an inclination of the head to pass out of the room before him, and remained silent. I had no resource but to comply.

When we reached the door, the child, setting down the candle, turned to say good night, and raised her face to kiss me. Then she ran to the old man, who folded her in his arms and bade God bless her.

"Sleep soundly, Nell," he said in a low voice," and angels guard thy bed. Do not forget thy prayers, my sweet."

"No, indeed," answered the child, fervently; "they make me feel so happy."

"That's well; I know they do; they should," said the old man. "Bless thee a hundred times!' Early in the morning I shall be home."

"You'll not ring twice," returned the child. "The bell wakes me even in the middle of a dream."

With this they separated. The child opened the door (now guarded by a shutter which I had heard the boy put up before he left the house), and with another farewell, whose clear and tender note I have recalled a thousand times, held it until we had passed out. The old man paused a moment while it was gently closed and fastened on the inside, and, satisfied that this was done, walked on at a slow pace. At the street corner he stopped. Regarding me with a troubled countenance, he said that our ways were widely different, and that he must take his leave. I would have spoken, but summoning up more alacrity than might have been expected in one of his appearance, he hurried away. I could see that, twice or thrice, he looked back as if to ascertain if I were still watching him, or perhaps to assure himself that I was not following at a distance. The obscurity of the night favored his disappearance, and his figure was soon beyond my sight.

I remained standing on the spot where he had left me, unwilling to depart, and yet unknowing why I should loiter there. I looked wistfully into the street we had lately quitted, and, after a time, directed my steps that way. I passed and repassed the house, and stopped and listened at the door; all was dark and silent as the grave.

Yet I lingered about, and could not tear myself away; thinking of all possible harm that might happen to the child of fires, and robberies, and even murder and feeling as if some evil must ensue if I turned my back upon the place. The closing of a door or window in the street, brought me before the curiosity dealer's once more. I crossed the road, and looked up at the house, to assure myself that the noise had not come from there. No, it was black, cold, and lifeless as before.

There were few passengers astir; the street was sad and dismal, and pretty well my own. A few stragglers from the theeters hurried by, and, now and then, I turned aside to avoid some noisy drunkard as he reeled homeward; but these interruptions were not frequent, and soon ceased. The clock struck one. Still I paced up and down, promising myself that every time should be the last, and breaking faith with myself on some new plan, as often as I did so.

The more I thought of what the old man had said, and of his looks and bearing, the less I could account for what I had seen and heard. I had a strong misgiving that his nightly absence was for no good purpose. I had only come to know the fact through the innocencence of the child; and though the old man was by at the time and saw my undisguised surprise, he had preserved a strange mystery on the subject and offered no word of explanation. These reflections naturally recalled again, more strongly than before, his haggard face, his wandering manner, his restless, anxious looks. His affection for the child might not be inconsistant with villainy of the worst kind; even that very affection was in itself an extraordinary contradiction, or how could he leave her thus? Disposed as I was to think badly of him. I never doubted that his love for her was real. I could not admit the thought, remembering what had passed between us, and the tone of voice in which he had called her by her name.

"Stay here, of course," the child had said, in answer to my question, "I always do." What could take him from home by night, and every night? I called up all the strange tales I had ever heard, of dark and secret deeds committed in great towns, and escaping detection for a long series of years. Wild as many of these stories were, I could not find one adapted to this mystery, which only became the more impenetrable, in proportion as I sought to solve it.

Occupied with such thoughts as these, and a crowd of others all tending to the same point, I continued to pace the street for two long hours. At length, the rain began to descend heavily; and then, overpowered by fatigue, though no less interested than I had been at first, I engaged the nearest coach and so got home. A cheerful fire was blazing on the hearth, the lamp burned brightly, my clock received me with its old familiar welcome; everything was quiet, warm and cheering, and in happy contrast to the gloom and darkness I had quitted.

I sat down in my easy chair, and falling back upon its ample cushions, pictured to myself the child in her bed; alone, unwatched, uncared for (except by angels), yet sleeping peacefully. So very young, so spiritual, so slight and fairy-like a

creature passing the long dull nights in such an uncongenial
place. I could not dismiss it from my thoughts.

We are so much in the habit of allowing impressions to be
made upon us by external objects,which should be produced by
reflection alone,but which,without such visible aids,often escape us,that I am not sure I should have been so thoroughly
possessed by this one subject,but for the heaps of fantastic
things I had seen huddled together in the curiosity dealer's
warehouse. These crowding on my mind,in connection with the
child,and gathering around her,as it were,brought her condi-
tion palpably before me. I had her image,without any effort
of imagination,surrounded and beset by everything that was foreign to its nature,and furthest removed from the sympathies
of her sex and age. If these helps to my fancy had all been
wanting,and I had been forced to imagine her in a common chamber,with nothing unusual or uncouth in its appearance,it is
very probable that I should have been less impressed with her
strange and solitary state. As it was,she seemed to exist in
a kind of allegory; and,having these shapes about her,claimed
my interest so strongly,that (as I have already remarked) I
could not dismiss her from my recollection,do what I would.

"It would be a curious speculation," said I,after some
restless turns across and across the room,"to imagine her in
her future life,holding her solitary way among a crowd of wild
grotesque companions; the only pure,fresh,youthful object in
the throng. It would be curious to find--"

I checked myself here,for the theme was carrying me along
with it at a great pace,and I already saw before me a region
on which I was little disposed to enter. I agreed with myself that this was idle musing,and resolved to go to bed,and
court forgetfulness.

But all that night,waking or in my sleep,the same thoughts
occurred,and the same images retained possession of my brain
I had ever before me,the old dark murky rooms--the gaunt suits
of mail with their ghostly silent air--the faces all awry,grin-
ning from wood and stone--the dust,and rust,and worm that
lives in wood--and alone in the midst of all this lumber and
decay and ugly age,the beautiful child in her gentle slumber,
smiling through her light and sunny dreams.